toys to crochet

Claire Garland

POTTER CRAFT

NEW YORK

Published in the United States by Potter Craft, an
imprint of the Crown Publishing Group, a division of
Random House, Inc., New York.

www.crownpublishing.com
www.pottercraft.com

POTTER CRAFT and CLARKSON N. POTTER are
trademarks, and POTTER and colophon are registered
trademarks of Random House, Inc.

Originally published in hardcover in Great Britain by
Collins & Brown, an imprint of Anova Books Company
Ltd., London.

Library of Congress Cataloging-in-Publication Data

Garland, Claire.
   Toys to crochet / Claire Garland. — 1st ed.
         p. cm.
   Includes bibliographical references and index.
   ISBN 978–0–307–38306–8 (trade pbk. : alk. paper)
   1.   Soft toy making. 2.   Crocheting.   I. Title.
   TT174.3.G35 2007
   745.592'4—dc22
2007007063

Printed in China

Commissioning Editor: Michelle Lo
Design Manager: Gemma Wilson
Assistant Editor: Katie Hudson
Design Studios: Ben Cracknell
Photographer: Mark Winwood
Senior Production Controller: Morna McPherson
Cover design by Amy Sly

10 9 8 7 6 5 4 3 2 1

First American Edition

Potter Craft Newsletter:
Sign up for our monthly newsletter at
www.pottercraftnews.com to get information about
new books, receive free patterns, and enter contests
to win free prizes.

Contents

Introduction

I've always found crochet to be a craft of myriad benefits. On a professional level, it's a design tool that provides ease and workability—after all, what other craft allows one to create perfect circles in a matter of a few simple knots? On a personal note, crocheting is a stress-reliever and the perfect way to unwind after a long day. With just a hook and a ball of yarn, crocheting offers an immediate sense of accomplishment and release, especially when creating toys.

My creative inspiration is sparked by my children—I observe the way they create miniature worlds and how their toys develop into "lovable friends" and "cuddly beasts." My objective in this book was to create a collection of unique and character-driven toys, like the pint-sized projects in *Toys to Knit* and *Toys to Sew*. The results, I hope, are fun creations that are totally endearing.

I couldn't possibly choose a favorite from the projects—they all brim with personality, and I love them equally. The Mermaid, with her cascading mane and long, crocheted fin, radiates beauty; the Marmoset, in his red overalls, is always up for mischief; and George the Shark may *look* mean, but he's really a soft-hearted guy.

All the projects in *Toys to Crochet* are easy to make and require very little time to finish, which is great when you have an anxious child peering over your shoulder. (I recommend stitching up a couple of finger puppets for such an occasion!)

I hope the projects in this book bring as much satisfaction to you as they have for me. I thoroughly enjoyed designing and making each toy, and I hope I've managed to express this pleasure on every page.

Enjoy and get hooked!

Dolls &
Doll Clothes

This chapter contains patterns for a doll, a basic bear with a variety of clothes, and several adorable accessories. Once you have conquered the basics, take your pick from this collection of lovable projects.

Basic Bear

This classic bear can be crocheted up without a hitch. Use him as the foundation for Sailor Bear (page 27)—or combine him with other basic clothes to create your own unique teddy.

FINISHED SIZE
12¼ in (31 cm) tall × 13¾ in (35 cm) wide (arms outstretched)

MATERIALS
- Karabella *Aurora Bulky*
  One ball Beige 22 (MC)
- Hook: H-8 (5.00 mm)
- Black embroidery thread for attaching beads and for mouth
- Two ¼ in (6 mm) black glass pearls or similar for eyes
- Dark blue embroidery thread for nose
- Polyester toy fiberfill or batting
- Yarn needle

GAUGE
9 sts and 8 rnds measured over 2 in (5 cm) working single crochet in MC and using H-8 (5.00 mm) hook.

NOTE:
Before beg the second rnd in each section, place a marker or short length of contrasting yarn across your crochet and up against the loop on the hook and above the working yarn. Work Rnd 2 then slip the marker out and place it at the beg of the next rnd and so on. The marker will indicate where each subsequent rnd starts.

HEAD
Foundation row: Beg at the nose end and using MC, make 2ch.
Rnd 1: 8sc in 2nd ch from hook.
Rnd 2: [1sc in each of next 2sc, 2sc in next sc] twice, 1sc in each of next 2sc (10 sc).
Rnd 3: 1sc in each sc around.
Shape top of nose
Rnd 4: [1sc in each of next 2sc, 2sc in next sc) 3 times, 1sc in next sc (13 sc).
Rnd 5: 1sc in each sc around.
Rnd 6: *2sc in each sc around (26 sc).
Rnd 7: 1sc in each sc around.
Rnd 8: [1sc in each of next 3sc, 2sc in next sc] 5 times, 1sc in next 6sc (31 sc).
Rnd 9: 1sc in each sc around.
Shape back of head
Rnd 10: Skip first sc, *1sc in each of next 4sc, skip next sc, rep from * to end (24 sc).
Rnd 11: 1sc in each sc around.
Rnd 12: *1sc in each of next 3sc, skip next sc, rep from * to end (18 sc).
Rnd 13: *1sc in each of next 2sc, skip next sc, rep from * to end (12 sc).
Turn out to RS. Stuff the head lightly.

Rnd 14: *1sc in next sc, skip next sc, rep from * to end (6 sc).
Rep last row until gap is closed. Fasten off. Weave in end.

EARS
Make 2 alike.
Foundation row: Beg at the ear base and using MC, make 2ch.
Row 1: 6sc in 2nd ch from hook, turn.
Row 2: 1ch, 1sc in top half of each sc along.
Fasten off, leaving a tail end long enough with which to hand-sew the ears onto the head.

BODY
Foundation row: Beg at the bottom and using MC, make 4ch, join with sl st at the top of first ch to make a ring.
Rnd 1: 12hdc in ring.
Rnd 2: 1hdc in each hdc around.
Rnd 3: *1hdc in next hdc, 2hdc in next hdc, rep from * to end (18 hdc).
Rnd 4: 1hdc in each hdc around.
Rep last 2 rnds once more (27 hdc).
Rnd 7: 1hdc in each hdc around.
Shape back
Rnd 8: [1hdc in next hdc, skip next hdc]

5 times, 1hdc in each of next 17 hdc
(22 hdc).

Rnd 9: [1hdc in next hdc, skip next hdc]
4 times, 1hdc in each of next 11 hdc
(18 hdc).

Rnd 10: 1hdc in each hdc around.
Rep last rnd once more.

Rnd 12: *1hdc in next hdc, skip next
hdc, rep from * to end (9 hdc).
Stuff the body.

Rnd 13: *1hdc in each of next 2hdc, skip
next hdc, rep from * to end (6 hdc).
Fasten off, leaving a tail end long
enough to join the body to the head.

ARMS

Make 2 alike.

Foundation row (RS): Beg at the top of
the arm and using MC, make 21ch.

Row 1 (WS): 1sc in 2nd ch from hook,
1sc in each ch to end, turn (20 sc).

Row 2 (RS): 1ch, 1sc in each sc to end,
turn (20 sc).
Rep last row 3 times more.

Shape hand

Row 6 (RS): 1ch, 1sc in each of next 6sc,
turn.

Row 7 (WS): 1ch, skip next sc, 1sc in
each sc across, turn (5 sc).

Row 8 (RS): 1ch, skip next sc, 1sc in each sc across, turn (4 sc).

Row 9 (WS): 1ch, skip next sc, 1sc in next sc, skip next sc, 1sc in next sc (3 sc). Fasten off, leaving a tail end long enough for you to sew the arm seam.

Join other half of hand

With RS facing and working along foundation row edge, count in 6ch from hand end, pull though yarn MC to 6th ch, 1ch, 1sc in each ch to end (6 sc).

Row 2 (WS): 1ch, skip next sc, 1sc in each sc across, turn (5 sc).

Row 3 (RS): 1ch, skip next sc, 1sc in each sc across, turn (4 sc).

Row 4 (WS): 1ch, skip next sc, 1sc in next sc, skip next sc, 1sc in next sc (2 sc). Fasten off.

LEGS

Make 2 alike.

Foundation row: Beg at toe and using MC, make 2ch.

Rnd 1: 6sc in 2nd ch from hook.

Rnd 2: *1sc in next sc, 2sc in next sc, rep from * around (9 sc).

Rnd 3: 1sc in each sc around. Rep last rnd 5 times more.

Shape heel

Row 9: 1sc in each of next 4sc, turn.

Row 10: 1ch, 1sc in each of next 4sc, turn. Rep last row once more.

Fasten off. Join heel seam—fold the finishing row (last 4sc) in half so that the two ends meet and sew together to form back of heel.

Shape top of foot

Rnd 1: Join in yarn MC with a sl st at top of heel seam, work 4sc along 1st row-end edge of heel, 1sc in each of 5sc across front of foot, then 4sc along 2nd row-end edge of heel (13 sc).

Rnd 2: 1sc in each of next 13sc.

Shape ankle

Rnd 3: [1sc in each of next 3sc, skip next sc] 3 times, 1sc in next sc (10 sc).

Rnd 4: 1sc in each of next 10sc. Rep last rnd until the leg measures 7½ in (19 cm) from toe. Fasten off.

TO FINISH

Referring to the photograph for the positioning of eyes, hand sew a bead on either side of the nose. Using dark blue embroidery thread, hand sew the nose with a few horizontal stitches. Sew a mouth using six strands of black embroidery thread by securing a length of thread at the corner of the mouth position at the back of the face, bring the thread to the front, re-inserting at the length you want the mouth to be. Sew a short stitch in the middle of the stitched line, securing the stitch down.

Stuff the body fairly firmly. Close the gap at the bottom. Hand sew the head to the body. Over-sew the arms to join, stuffing the hands lightly.

Stuff the feet. Sew the arms to the side of the body and the legs to the bottom. Sew the ears to the top of the head.

If liked, you can hand sew a button that is small enough to go through a sc stitch yet large enough to be secure, about ⅜ in (10 mm) in diameter, onto the back of the bear around the waist—this will help to hold up the trousers, pants, and skirt.

Basic Doll

This pattern is the foundation for all dolls in the book. Dress her in the basic clothes (page 16) or sun clothes (page 21)—a stylish ensemble proves that being short on stature doesn't mean being short on taste!

FINISHED SIZE
16½ in (42 cm) tall × 19¾ in (50 cm) wide (arms outstretched)

MATERIALS
- **Rooster Yarns *Almerino DK***
  One ball Cornish 201 (MC)
- **DK/medium (light worsted/worsted weight)**
  One ball in a suitable color for hair (A)
- **Debbie Bliss *Baby Cashmerino***
  One ball Baby Blue 340204 for tankini (B)
- Hooks: E-4 (3.50 mm) and G-6 (4.00 mm)
- Small pieces of felt for eyes
- Black thread for sewing on eyes
- Two ¼ in (6 mm) black glass beads or similar for eyes
- Pink embroidery thread for sewing mouth
- Polyester toy fiberfill or batting
- Yarn needle

GAUGE
For doll: 12 sts and 12 rnds measured over 2 in (5 cm) working single crochet in MC and using E-4 (3.50 mm) hook.

For undergarments: 9 sts and 10 rows measured over 2 in (5 cm) working single crochet in B and using G-6 (4.00 mm) hook.

NOTE:
Before beg the second rnd in each section, place a marker or short length of contrasting yarn across your crochet and up against the loop on the hook and above the working yarn. Work Rnd 2 then slip the marker out and place it at the beg of the next rnd and so on. The marker will indicate where each subsequent rnd starts.

HEAD & BODY
Make back and front alike.
Foundation row: Using yarn MC and E-4 (3.50 mm) hook, beg at the base, make 13ch.
Row 1: 1sc in 2nd ch from hook, 1sc in each ch across, turn (12 sc).
Row 2: 2ch, 1sc in 2nd ch from hook, 1sc in each sc to last sc, 2sc in last sc, turn (14 sc).
Row 3: 1ch, 1sc in each sc across, turn.
Rep last 2 rows twice more (18 sc).

Row 8: 1ch, 1sc in each of next 18 sc, turn (18 sc).
Rep last row 8 times more.
Shape body and neck
Row 17: 1ch, skip first sc, 1sc in each sc to last 2sc, skip next sc, 1sc in last sc, turn (16 sc).
Rep last row 3 times more (10 sc).
Row 21: 1ch, 1sc in each sc across, turn (10 sc).
Rep last row 5 times more.
Shape head
Row 27: 2ch, 1sc in 2nd ch from hook, 1sc in each sc to last sc, 2sc in last sc, turn (12 sc).
Rep last row twice more (16 sc).
Row 30: 1ch, 1sc in each sc across, turn (16 sc).
Rep last row 3 times more.
Shape top of head
Row 34: 1ch, skip first sc, 1sc in each sc to last 2sc, skip next sc, 1sc in last sc, turn (14 sc).
Rep last row 4 times more (6 sc).
Fasten off.

ARMS
Make 2 alike.
Foundation row: Using yarn MC and E-4 (3.50 mm) hook, make 38ch.
Row 1: 1sc in 2nd ch from hook, 1sc in each ch across, turn (37 sc).

Row 2: 1ch, 1sc in each sc across, turn (37 sc).
Rep last row twice more.
Fasten off, leaving a long tail end—use this to over-sew along the foundation and finishing rows to join.

FEET & LEGS
Make 2 alike.
Foundation row: Using yarn MC and E-4 (3.50 mm) hook, beg at toe, make 2ch.
Rnd 1: 6sc in 2nd ch from hook.
Rnd 2: *1sc in next sc, 2sc in next sc, rep from * around (9 sc).
Rnd 3: 1sc in each of next 9sc.
Rep last rnd 5 times more.
Shape heel
Row 1: 1sc in each of next 4sc, turn.
Row 2: 1ch, 1sc in each of next 4sc, turn.
Rep last row once more.
Fasten off. Join heel seam—fold the finishing row (last 4sc) in half so that the two ends meet and sew together to form back of heel.
Shape top of foot
Rnd 1: Join in yarn MC with a sl st at top of heel seam, work 4sc along first row-end edge of heel, 1sc in each of 5sc across front of foot, then 4sc along 2nd row-end edge of heel (13 sc).
Rnd 2: 1sc in each of next 13sc.

Shape ankle
Rnd 3: [1sc in each of next 3sc, skip next sc] 3 times, 1sc in last sc, turn (10 sc).
Stuff foot
Rnd 4: 1sc in each of next 10sc.
Rep last rnd until the leg measures 9 in (23 cm) from toe.
Fasten off.

TO FINISH
Cut out two circles from felt ⅜ in (10 mm) in diameter for the irises. Sew a bead to the center of each iris. Referring to the photograph for positioning, sew the eyes to the face. Sew a mouth using 6 strands of pink embroidery thread by securing a length of yarn at the corner of the mouth position at the back of the face and bring the yarn to the front, re-inserting at desired mouth length. Sew a short stitch in the middle of the stitched line, securing the stitch down a little to form the bottom lip. Work another stitch above this "caught" stitch to form the upper lip.
Using a blunt-ended yarn needle and yarn MC, join the front of the body to the back, leaving the bottom edge open for stuffing. Stuff the doll firmly in the head, and very lightly in the trunk. Close the gap at the bottom.

Over-sew the arms to join. Sew the arms to the side of the body.

Sew the legs to the bottom of the body. To sew on hair, cut yarn A into lengths of 14¼ in (36 cm). Taking one length at a time, bend in half and, using a crochet hook, pull the loop through a sc stitch at the top of the head, referring to the photograph for hair placement. Pass the cut ends through the loops, then pull the cut ends firmly so that the knot lies at the top of the head. Continue with this fringing technique along the top and a little way down the back of the head depending on how thick you want the hair to be.

Tankini

BOTTOM

Foundation row: Using yarn B and G-6 (4.00 mm) hook, make 33ch.
Row 1: 1sc in 2nd ch from hook, 1sc in each ch across, turn (32 sc).
Row 2: 1ch, 1sc in each of next 32sc, join into ring with sl st in first sc, taking care not to twist the rows (32 sc).
Cont to work in rnds.
Rnd 1: 1sc in each sc around (32 sc).
Rep last rnd twice more.
Shape front
Row 1: 1sc in each of next 12sc, turn (12 sc).

Row 2: 1ch, 1sc in each of next 12sc, turn.
Row 3: 1ch, skip first sc, 1sc in each of next 9sc, skip next sc, 1sc in last sc, turn (10 sc).
Row 4: 1ch, 1sc in each of next 10sc, turn (10 sc).
Row 5: 1ch, skip first sc, 1sc in each of next 7sc, skip next sc, 1sc in last sc, turn (8 sc).
Row 6: 1ch, 1sc in each of next 8sc, turn (8 sc).
Row 7: 1ch, skip first sc, 1sc in each of next 5sc, skip next sc, 1sc in last sc, turn (6 sc).
Row 8: 1ch, 1sc in each of next 6sc, turn (6 sc).
Row 9: 1ch, skip first sc, 1sc in each of next 3sc, skip next sc, 1sc in last sc, turn (4 sc).
Row 10: 1ch, 1sc in each of next 4sc (4 sc).
Fasten off, leaving a long tail end for sewing up the gusset seam.
Shape back
Row 1: With RS facing, join in yarn B to first of 20 rem sc at left back, 1ch, skip sc where yarn was joined, 1sc in each of next 17sc, skip next sc, 1sc in last sc, turn (18 sc).
Row 2: 1ch, skip first sc, 1sc in each to last sc, skip last sc, turn (16 sc).
Rep last row 6 times more, turn (4 sc).

Row 9: 1ch, 1sc in each of next 4sc. Fasten off, weave in loose end.

TO FINISH

With RS facing and matching yarn, sew up the short waist seam and gusset seam, leaving the legs open.

TOP

Foundation row: Using yarn B and G-6 (4.00 mm) hook, make 18ch, turn.
Row 1: 1sc in 2nd ch from hook, 1sc in each ch across, turn (17 sc).
Row 2: 1ch, 1sc in each of next 17sc, turn.
Row 3: 1ch, 1 sc in first sc, *skip 1sc, 5dc in next sc, skip 1sc, 1sc in next sc, rep from * to end.
Fasten off.
For the back strap, make a chain long enough to fit across the back and sew to row-ends of the top.
For each shoulder strap, make a chain long enough to fit over the shoulders. Sew one end of each strap to the foundation row of the top and the other end to the back strap.

Basic Clothes

A fashionable girl-about-town needs a chic urban wardrobe to reflect her unique personality. Many of these garments are the basics for other doll clothes within this chapter. A hat and striped culottes look fabulous day and night while a button-up hoodie is ideal outerwear when temperatures drop.

Hooded Cardigan

FINISHED SIZE
8 × 9½ in (20 × 24 cm) from bottom to tip of hood

MATERIALS
- **Sidar** *Snuggly DK*
  One ball of Lilac 219 (MC)
- **Anchor** *Tapisserie Wool*
  One ball of Damson 8512 for button band (A)
- Hook: H-8 (5.00 mm)
- Three ¾ in (18 mm) buttons
- Yarn needle

GAUGE
9 sts and 7 rows measured over 2 in (5 cm) working single crochet in MC and using H-8 (5.00 mm) hook.

NOTE:
Before beg the second rnd in each section, place a marker or short length of contrasting yarn across your crochet and up against the loop on the hook and above the working yarn. Work Rnd 2 then slip the marker out and place it at the beg of the next rnd and so on. The marker will indicate where each subsequent rnd starts.

FRONT

Foundation row: Beg at right center front, and using yarn A, make 12ch.

Row 1 (RS): 2sc in 2nd ch from hook, 1sc in each ch across, turn (12 sc).

Row 2: 1ch, 1sc in first sc, (skip next 2sc, make buttonhole by making 2ch, 1sc in each of next 2sc) twice, skip next 2sc, make 2ch, 2sc in last sc, turn (13 sts).

Row 3: Join in yarn MC with a sl st in last sc of previous row, 1ch, 2sc in first sc, 1sc in next sc, 2sc in next 2ch sp, (1sc in each of next 2sc, 2sc in next 2ch sp) twice, 1sc in last sc, turn (14 sc).

Row 4: 1ch, 1sc in each sc across, turn.

Row 5: 1ch, 2sc in first sc, 1sc in each sc across, turn (15 sc).

Row 6: 1ch, 1sc in each sc across, turn. Rep last row 3 times more.

Make right armhole

Row 10 (WS): 1ch, 1sc in each of next 6sc, skip next 7sc, make 7ch, 1sc in each of next 2sc, turn.

Make back

Row 11 (RS): 1ch, 1sc in each of next 2sc, 1sc in each of next 7ch, 1sc in each of next 6sc, turn.

Row 12: 1ch, 1sc in each sc across, turn. Rep last row 8 times more.

Make left armhole

Row 21 (RS): 1ch, 1sc in each of next 2sc, skip next 7sc, make 7ch, 1sc in each of next 6sc, turn.

Row 22: 1ch, 1sc in each of next 6sc, 1sc in each of next 7ch, 1sc in each of next 2sc, turn (15 sc).

Row 23: 1ch, 1sc in each sc across, turn. Rep last row 3 times more.

Row 27 (RS): Sl st in first sc, 1ch, 1sc in each sc across, turn (14 sc).

Row 28: 1ch, 1sc in each sc to last sc, skip last sc, turn (13 sc). Rep last 2 rows once more.

Row 31 (RS): Sl st in first sc, 1ch, 1sc in each sc across (10 sc). Fasten off.

SLEEVES

Make 2 alike.

Rnd 1: With RS facing, join yarn MC with a sl st into a sc at base of armhole and drawing a loop through, make 1ch, 1sc in each sc along edges of armhole, join with sl st in top of first sc, turn (14 sc).

Rnd 2: Working from the inside of the cardigan, 1ch, 1sc in each of next 14 sc.

Rep last rnd until the entire sleeve—from Rnd 1—measures 3 in (8 cm), ending with a sl st in top of first sc.

Fasten off and weave in ends.

HOOD

Row 1: With RS facing, join on MC with a sl st into the sc at beg of right center front and drawing a loop through make 1ch, work 30sc along neck edge to left center front, turn.

Row 2: Sl st in first sc, 1ch, 1sc in each next 27sc, skip next sc, 1sc in last sc, turn (28 sc).

Row 3: 1ch, 1sc in each sc across, turn.

Row 4: Sl st in first sc, 1ch, 1sc in each of next 25sc, skip next sc, 1sc in last sc, turn (26 sc).

Row 5: 1ch, 1sc in each sc across, turn.

Row 6: Sl st in first sc, 1ch, 1sc in each of next 23sc, skip next sc, 1sc in last sc, turn (24 sc).

Row 7: 1ch, 1sc in each sc across, turn.

Rep last row 4 times more.

Row 12: 1ch, 1sc in each of next 11sc, [2sc in next sc] twice, 1sc in each of next 11sc, turn (26 sc).

Row 13: 1ch, 1sc in each sc across, turn.

Row 14: 1ch, 1sc in each of next 12sc, [2sc in next sc] twice, 1sc in each of next 12sc, turn (28 sc).

Row 15: 1ch, 1sc in each sc across, turn.

Row 16: 1ch, 1sc in each of next 13sc, [2sc in next sc] twice, 1sc in each of next 13sc, turn (30 sc).

Row 17: 1ch, 1sc in each sc across, turn.

Row 18: 1ch, 1sc in each of next 14sc, [2sc in next sc] twice, 1sc in each of next 14sc, turn (32 sc).

Row 19: 1ch, 1sc in each sc across.

Fasten off, leaving a tail end long enough to sew up the seam with. With RS facing,

sew up the hood along the finishing row. Weave in end.

HOOD EDGING

With RS facing, join in yarn A with a sl st into the last sc worked at end of buttonband and drawing a loop through make 1ch, 1sc in each row-end edge along hood edge to left center front, ending in sl st in top of last sc. Fasten off.

Basic Trousers

FINISHED SIZE

6¾ in (17 cm) long and 9 in (23 cm) diameter around waist

MATERIALS

- **Rooster *Almerino DK***
  One ball of Caviar 206 (MC)
  One ball of Hazelnut 202 (A)
- Hook size: H-8 (5.00 mm)
- 12 in (30 cm) × ¼ in (6 mm) ribbon for waist tie

GAUGE

8 sts and 9 rows measured over 2 in (5 cm) working single crochet in MC and using H-8 (5.00 mm) hook.

TROUSERS

Follow this color sequence throughout the pattern:
Foundation row and row 1—yarn MC
Rows 2 and 3—yarn A
Rows 4 and 5—yarn MC
Rows 6 and 7—yarn A, and so on.
Foundation row: Using yarn MC, beg at the leg end, make 27ch.
Row 1: 1sc in 2nd ch from hook, 1sc in each ch across, turn (26 sc).
Row 2: 1ch, 1sc in each sc across, turn. Rep last row once more.
Row 4: 1ch, 1sc in each sc across, turn,

join into a ring with a sl st in first sc of row, taking care not to twist the rows—cont to work in rnds as follows:
Rnd 1: 1ch, 1sc in each of next 26sc around, join with a sl st in first sc of row (26 sc).
Rnd 2: 1sc in each of next 26sc.
Rep last rnd until the entire leg measures 4¼ in (11 cm), turn.
Now work in rows.
Leg shaping
Next row: 1ch, skip next sc, 1sc in each sc to end (marker), turn (25 sc).
Rep last row 8 times more (17 sc).
Next row: 1ch, 1sc in each sc across.
Fasten off.
Make another leg in the same way.
Join legs
With WS out, join two legs at back and front gusset by working 1sc in each row-end edge from waist at center front, down along center front up along center back to center back waist. Turn out to RS.
Waistband
At waist edge, join in yarn A to a sc at center back waist edge, work 1ch, 1sc in each sc around waist (34 sc).
Next rnd: 1sc in each sc around, sl st to first sc of rnd.
Fasten off.

TO FINISH

Weave in all ends. Thread the ribbon

through waistband through first sc after center front seam, then every 3rd sc around waistband.

Basic Shoes

FINISHED SIZE
3¼ in (8 cm) long

MATERIALS
- RYC *Cashsoft 4 ply*
  One ball of Dive 427
- Hook size: E-4 (3.50 mm)
- Two ³⁄₁₆ in (5 mm) buttons
- Blue thread for attaching buttons

GAUGE
9 sts and 10 rows measured over 2 in (5 cm) working single crochet in MC and using E-4 (3.50 mm) hook.

SHOES
Make 2 alike.
Foundation row: Beg at toe, make 2ch.
Rnd 1: 6sc in 2nd ch from hook.
Rnd 2: 2sc in each of next 6sc (12 sc).
Rnd 3: *1sc in each of next 2sc, 2sc in next sc, rep from * around (16 sc).
Rnd 4: 1sc in each of next 16sc.
Rep last rnd twice more.
Shape top of shoe
Rnd 7: [Skip next sc, 1sc in next sc] 4 times, 1sc in each of next 8sc, turn (12 sc).

Now work in rows.
Shape upper
Row 1: 1ch, 1sc in each of next 6sc, turn.
Row 2: 1ch, 2sc in first sc, 1sc in each of next 3sc, 2sc in next sc, 1sc in last sc, turn (8 sc).
Row 3: 1ch, 2sc in first sc, 1sc in each of next 5sc, 2sc in next sc, 1sc in last sc, turn (10 sc).
Row 4: 1ch, 2sc in first sc, 1sc in each of next 7sc, 2sc in next sc, 1sc in last sc, turn (12 sc).
Row 5: 1ch, 1sc in each of next 12sc, turn.
Rep last row twice more.
Next rnd: 1sc in first sc of this row to join back of heel. Starting at heel, work 21sc evenly around upper edge of shoe, sl st in first sc of rnd.
Fasten off.
Sew up heel seam. Weave in ends.

SHOE STRAPS
Make 2 alike.
Foundation row: Make 10ch.
Row 1: 1sc in 2nd ch from hook, 1sc in each ch across (9 sc).
Fasten off, leaving tail ends long enough for sewing onto the shoe.

TO FINISH
Join one side of the strap to sc at upper shaping. Sew the other side of the strap in place with a button.

Basic Skirt

FINISHED SIZE
2¾ in (7 cm) long and 7¾ in (20 cm) diameter around waist

MATERIALS
- **Debbie Bliss** *Cotton Denim Aran*
  One ball of Denim Blue 14503 (MC)
- Hook: K-10½ (6.50 mm)
- One ⅓ in (8 mm) button
- Three ³⁄₁₆ in (5 mm) buttons for decoration (optional)
- Thread for attaching buttons

GAUGE
7 sts and 6½ rows measured over 2 in (5 cm) working single crochet in MC and using K-10½ (6.50 mm) hook.

SKIRT
Foundation row: Beg at the waist edge, make 24ch, turn.
Row 1: 1sc in 2nd ch from hook, 1sc in each ch across, turn (23 sc).
Row 2: 1ch, 1sc in each sc across, do not twist yarn, join with sl st in 1ch to form a ring. Now work in rows.
Rnd 1: 1sc in each sc around (23 sc).
Rnd 2: 1sc in each of next 23sc.
Rep last rnd 5 times more, ending sl st in next sc.
Fasten off.

TO FINISH

At each side of the skirt at waist, pinch in 2sc to wrong side and catch them with a couple of stitches to create a dart. Sew a button at the back that is just large enough for a stitch to fasten over it and be secure.

Sew the three smaller buttons evenly down the front (optional).

Basic Hat

FINISHED SIZE

4¼ in (11 cm) diameter

MATERIALS

- **RYC** *Cashsoft Aran*
  One ball of Bud 006 (MC)
- **Adriafil** *Angora Carezza*
  Small amount of Pink for brim (A)
- Hook: H-8 (5.00 mm)

GAUGE

9 sts and 8 rnds measured over 2 in (5 cm) working single crochet in MC and using H-8 (5.00 mm) hook.

HAT

The crown and the brim are worked as one.

Foundation row: Beg at top of crown, using yarn MC, make 2ch.

Rnd 1: 6sc in 2nd ch from hook.

Rnd 2: 2sc in each of next 6sc (12 sc).

Rnd 3: *1sc in next sc, 2sc in next sc, rep from * around (18 sc).

Rnd 4: *1sc in each of next 2sc, 2sc in next sc, rep from * around (24 sc).

Rnd 5: *1sc in each of next 3sc, 2sc in next sc, rep from * around (30 sc).

Rnd 6: *1sc in each of next 4sc, 2sc in next sc, rep from * around (36 sc).

Shape sides

Rnd 7: 1dc in each of next 36sc.

Rnd 8: 1dc in each of next 36dc.

Fasten off yarn MC with sl st in next dc. Weave in end.

Brim

Join in yarn A with sl st in sl st of last rnd.

Rnd 9: *Skip next dc, 1dc in each of next 3dc, rep from * around (27 dc).

Rnd 10: [Skip next dc, 1dc in each of next 3dc] 6 times, skip next dc, 1 dc in each of last 2dc (20 dc).

Fasten off. Pull up center loose end to close the ring, weave in ends, leaving a short loop at center of hat.

Sun Clothes

Let's go surfin'! Our toys love adventure and love to get out when the sun is bright. A striped one-piece makes ideal sunbathing attire; a swimcap and flip-flops are stylish beach accessories.

Swimsuit

FINISHED SIZE
To fit Basic Doll or Bear (pages 10 and 13)

MATERIALS
- **Debbie Bliss** *Cashmerino Aran*
  Half a ball of pink 006 (MC)
- **RYC** *Cashsoft*
  Small amount of Dive 427 (A)
- Hook: H-8 (5.00 mm)
- Three ³/₁₆ in (5 mm) buttons for decoration (optional)
- Thread for attaching buttons

GAUGE
9 sts and 10 rnds measured over 2 in (5 cm) working single crochet in MC and using H-8 (5.00 mm) hook.

NOTE:
Before beg the second rnd in each section, place a marker or short length of contrasting yarn across your crochet and

up against the loop on the hook and above the working yarn. Work Rnd 2 then slip the marker out and place it at the beg of the next rnd and so on. The marker will indicate where each subsequent rnd starts.

SWIMSUIT FRONT & BACK
Foundation rnd: Beg at the top of the costume, using MC, make 22ch, taking care not to twist the chain join with a sl st in first ch to form ring.
Rnd 1: 1sc in each ch around (22 sc).

Rnd 2: 1sc in each sc around.
Rep last rnd twice more, fasten off yarn MC with sl st in next sc.
Rnd 5: Join in yarn A with sl st in same place as sl st of last rnd was worked, 1sc in each sc around.
Rnd 6: 1sc in each sc around.
Rep last rnd twice more, fasten off yarn A with sl st in next sc.
Join in yarn MC as rnd 5, then rep last 4 rnds in yarn MC once more, fasten off yarn MC with sl st in next sc.

Rnd 13: Join in yarn A with sl st in same place as sl st of last rnd was worked, 1sc in each of next 22sc, turn.

Now work in rows.

Shape front legs

Row 1: 1ch, 1sc in each of next 9sc, place marker, turn (9 sc).

Row 2: Sl st in first sc, 1ch, 1sc in each of next 7sc, skip last sc, turn (7 sc).

Row 3: Sl st in first sc, 1ch, 1sc in each of next 5sc, skip last sc, turn (5 sc).

Row 4: Sl st in first sc, 1ch, 1sc in each of next 3sc, skip last sc, turn (3 sc).

Row 5: 1ch, 1sc in each sc of next 3sc, turn.

Rep last row once more.

Fasten off.

Shape back legs

Row 1: At marker join in yarn A with sl st in next sc, 1sc in each of next 13sc, turn (13 sc).

Row 2: Sl st in first sc, 1ch, 1sc in each of next 11sc, skip last sc, turn (11 sc).

Row 3: Sl st in first sc, 1ch, 1sc in each of next 9sc, skip last sc, turn (9 sc).

Row 4: Sl st in first sc, 1ch, 1sc in each of next 7sc, skip last sc, turn (7 sc).

Row 5: Sl st in first sc, 1ch, 1sc in each of next 7sc, skip last sc, turn (5 sc).

Row 6: Sl st in first sc, 1ch, 1sc in each of next 7sc, skip last sc, turn (3 sc).

Fasten off.

Sew up the gusset then work border.

Border

Join on yarn MC with sl st in any sc around leg. Work in sc evenly around each leg.

Fasten off. Weave in ends.

STRAPS

Make 2 alike.

Using yarn A, make 11ch.

Row 1: 1sc in 2nd ch from hook, 1sc in each ch across (10 sc).

Fasten off. Weave in ends.

TO FINISH

At upper edge roll down the top to RS for 3 rows. Sew each strap to the inside of the costume behind the rolled over part—you may wish to dress the doll/bear in the swimsuit first to get the straps into position correctly before sewing in place. Sew buttons onto front of swimsuit.

Swim Cap

FINISHED SIZE

To fit Basic Doll or Bear (pages 10 and 13)

MATERIALS

- **Sirdar *Bonus DK***
  Small amount of Bright Orange (MC)
- **Opal *Uni 4ply***
  Small amount of Grass Green for flowers (A) (optional)
- Hook: H-8 (5.00 mm)
- One button
- Yarn needle

GAUGE

9 sts and 10 rnds measured over 2 in (5 cm) working single crochet in MC and using H-8 (5.00 mm) hook.

CAP

Foundation row: Beg at top of crown, using yarn MC, make 2ch.

Rnd 1: 6sc in 2nd ch from hook.

Rnd 2: 2sc in each of next 6sc (12 sc).

Rnd 3: *1sc in next sc, 2sc in next sc, rep from * around (18 sc).

Rnd 4: *1sc in each of next 2sc, 2sc in next sc, rep from * around (24 sc).

Rnd 5: *1sc in each of next 3sc, 2sc in next sc, rep from * around (30 sc).

Rnd 6: *1sc in each of next 4sc, 2sc in

next sc, rep from * around (36 sc).
Shape sides
NOTE: *For bear's hat only follow next two rnds to make gaps in side for ears— for dolls go straight to Rnd 9.*
Rnd 7: Skip first 5sc, make 5ch, 1sc in each of next 13sc, skip next 5sc, make 5ch, 1sc in each of next 13sc (36 sts).
Rnd 8: [1sc in each of next 5ch, 1sc in each of next 13sc] twice (36 sc).
Rnd 9: 1sc in each of next 36 sc.
Rep last rnd twice more for bear's hat and 4 times more for doll's hat.
Next rnd: *Skip next sc, 1sc in each of next 3sc, rep from * around (27 sc).
Next rnd: 1sc in each of next 27sc.
Rep last rnd twice more.
Fasten off. Weave in ends.

FIRST CHIN STRAP
Using yarn MC, make 7ch.
Row 1: 1sc in 2nd ch from hook, 1sc in each ch across (6 sc).
Fasten off.

SECOND CHIN STRAP
Using yarn MC, make 9ch.
Row 1: 1sc in 2nd ch from hook, skip next ch, make 1ch (to make buttonhole), 1 sc in each of next 6ch.
Fasten off.

FLORAL ADORNMENTS (OPTIONAL)
Using yarn A, make 4ch, sl st in first ch to form ring.
Rnd 1: 1ch, 7sc into ring, sl st in first ch of this rnd.
Rnd 2: [3ch, 3dc tog all in back loop of next sc, 3ch, 1sc into center ring, skip next sc] 4 times.
Fasten off.
Make as many or as few as you wish.

TO FINISH
Hand sew a chin strap to each side of the hat. Hand sew a button onto the first chin strap near the end not attached to the hat. Hand sew the flowers all over the hat.

Flip-Flops

FINISHED SIZE
To fit Basic Doll or Bear (pages 10 and 13)

MATERIALS
- **Opal** *Uni 4ply*
  Small amount of Grass Green (MC)
  Small amount of contrast color for toe bar (A)
- Hook: H-8 (5.00 mm)
- Yarn needle

GAUGE
9 sts and 10 rnds measured over 2 in (5 cm) working single crochet in MC and using H-8 (5.00 mm) hook.

SOLES
Make 2 alike.
Foundation row: Using MC, make 2ch.
Rnd 1: 4sc in 2nd ch from hook.
Rnd 2: *1sc in next ch, 2sc in next, rep from * once more (6sc).
Rnd 3: *1sc in next sc, 2sc in next, rep from * around (9sc).
Rnd 4: 1sc in each next sc.
Rep last rnd three times more.
Shape the heel
Flatten the sole down so that the last stitch work ends at the side of the shoe, work 1ch, then work 1sc across both thicknesses into each next 4sc, turn.
Next row: 1ch, 1sc in each next 4sc, turn.
Rep last row three times more, (or until the sole fits the length of your doll's/ bear's foot).
Fasten off. Weave in ends.

TOE BARS
Make 2 alike.
Using yarn A, make 16ch. Fasten off.

TO FINISH
Sew each loose end of the toe bar to halfway along the sole, join the center ch to the toe end.

Hula Hula Lula

Aloha! With her grass skirt and flowery lei, this Hawaiian doll brings a touch of paradise to any child's room. Sporting a red headband, a yellow orchid behind her ear and bangles, Lula loves to accessorize in color.

Doll

FINISHED SIZE
16½ in (42 cm) tall × 19¾ in (50 cm) wide (arms outstretched)

MATERIALS
- **Rooster *Almerino DK***
  One ball of Hazelnut 202 (MC)
- **Twilleys *Freedom Cotton DK***
  One ball of Cotton Black for hair (A)
- Hook: H-8 (3.50 mm)
- Small pieces of felt for eyes
- Black thread for sewing on eyes
- Two ¼ in (6 mm) black glass beads or similar for eyes
- Pink embroidery thread for mouth
- Polyester toy fiberfill or batting
- Yarn needle

GAUGE
9 sts and 9 rows measured over 2 in (5 cm) working single crochet in MC and using E-4 (5.00 mm) hook.

HEAD, BODY, ARMS, FEET, & LEGS
Using yarn MC and E-4 (3.50 mm) hook, make the same as for Basic Doll (page 13).

Wardrobe

MATERIALS
- **Sirdar *Snuggly DK***
  Small amount of Lilac 0219 (A)
- **GGH *Big Easy***
  Small amount of Turquoise 021 (B)
- **Lobster Pot *Bulky***
  Small amount of New Seagrass (C)
- **RYC *Cashcotton 4 Ply***
  Small amount of Sugar 901 (D)
- **Jaeger *Baby Merino 4 Ply***
  Small amount of Snowdrop 0102 (E)
- **Anchor *Tapisserie wool* various shades**—each sandal needs 1 skein
- Hook size: G-6 (4.00 mm)
- Three ³⁄₁₆ in (5 mm) buttons for decoration (optional)
- Thread for attaching button

GAUGE
12 sts and 10 rows measured over 2 in (5 cm) working single crochet in yarn A and using G-6 (4.00 mm) hook.

TANKINI BOTTOM
Using yarn A and G-6 (4.00 mm) hook, make the same as for Tankini Bottom (page 15).

TANKINI TOP
Foundation row: Using yarn D and G-6 (4.00 mm) hook, make 40ch.
Row 2: 1dc in 4th ch from hook, 1dc in each ch across, join with sl st in top of 3ch at beg of row to form ring, taking care not to twist the row (38 dc). Fasten off.
Rnd 1: Join in yarn E with sl st in last dc, 1sc in each dc around.
Rnd 2: 1sc in each sc around.
Rep last rnd once more.
Fasten off.

GRASS SKIRT
Foundation row: Using yarn B and G-6 (4.00 mm) hook, make 27ch.
Row 1: 1sc in 2nd ch from hook, 1sc in each ch across, turn (26 sc).
Row 2: 2ch (counts as 1ch and 1sc), miss first sc to make buttonhole—1sc in each sc to end.
Fasten off.
Sew on button at front.
To join "grass," cut 11 in (28 cm) lengths of yarn C. Taking one length at a time, bend in half and, using a crochet hook, pull the loop through a sc stitch along the foundation row of the skirt

waistband. Pass the cut ends through the loops then pull the cut ends firmly so that the knot lies close to the sc stitch. Continue with this fringing technique along the band.

LEI

Foundation row: Using any color for flower and G-6 (4.00 mm) hook, make 7ch, join with sl st to form ring.

Rnd 1: Working over the tail end, 14sc into ring, sl st in first sc of rnd.

Rnd 2: 4ch, (4tr tog, inserting hook twice in next sc and twice in foll sc, 3ch, 1sc in next sc, 3ch) 4 times, 4tr tog inserting hook as before, 3ch, sl st in first ch of rnd.

Fasten off. Draw up the center hole a little, leaving a tiny hole for threading. Weave in all ends.

Make as many flowers as you want for the lei and thread onto a single length of yarn.

HEADBAND

Foundation row: Using yarn E and G-6 (4.00 mm) hook, make 38ch.

Row 1: 1sc in 2nd ch from hook, 1sc in each ch across (37 sc).

Fasten off.

Sew up the row-end edges to join into a band. Weave in the ends.

SANDALS

Make 2 alike.

Sole

Foundation row: Using tapestry yarn and G-6 (4.00 mm) hook, make 13 ch.

Row 1: 1sc in 2nd ch from hook, 1sc in each ch across, turn (12 sc).

Row 2: 1ch, 1sc in each sc across, turn. Rep last row 7 times more.

Fasten off.

Fold into 3 layers across foundation and finishing rows, sew up to hold in place.

Upper strap

Foundation row: Using tapestry yarn and G-6 (4.00 mm) hook, make 9ch.

Row 1: 1sc in 2nd ch from hook, 1sc in each ch across, turn (8 sc).

Row 2: 1ch, 1sc in each sc across.

Fasten off.

Sew to each side of the sole a little more to the front than the back.

Sailor Bear

Ships ahoy! This little fella's had more than his fair share of excitement on the high seas. With his smart hat and tie, he's an invaluable treasure!

Sailor Bear

FINISHED SIZE
12¼ in (31 cm) tall × 13¾ in (35 cm) wide (arms outstretched)

MATERIALS
- **Brown Sheep Company *Lambs Pride Worsted***
  One ball of Cream M–10 (MC)
- Hook: H-8 (5.00 mm)
- Black embroidery thread for attaching beads and for mouth
- 12 in (30 cm) dark gray DK yarn for nose
- Two ¼ in (6 mm) black glass beads or similar for eyes
- Polyester toy fiberfill or batting
- Yarn needle

GAUGE
9 sts and 8 rnds measured over 2 in (5 cm) working single crochet in MC and using H-8 (5.00 mm) hook.

MATERIALS

- **Santos** *Denim*
  One ball of Denim (MC)
- **Jaeger** *Roma*
  One ball of Snow White 001 (A)
- Hook: H-8 (5.00 mm)

TROUSER
Make the same as Basic Trousers (see page 18) without following the color sequence used to create stripes. Use the following color sequence instead:
Foundation row and row 1—yarn MC
Row 2 onwards—yarn A
Continue in yarn A until you reach the waistband—change to yarn MC.

Sailor's Top

FINISHED SIZE
4¼ in (11 cm) long × 6 in (15 cm) wide

MATERIALS

- **Santos** *Denim*
  One ball of Denim (MC)
- **Jaeger** *Roma*
  One ball of Snow White 001 (A)
- Small amount of dark gray DK yarn for tie (B)
- Hook: H-8 (5.00 mm)
- Yarn needle

NOTE:

Before beg the second rnd in each section, place a marker or short length of contrasting yarn across your crochet and up against the loop on the hook and above the working yarn. Work Rnd 2 then slip the marker out and place it at the beg of the next rnd and so on. The marker will indicate where each subsequent rnd starts.

HEAD, BODY, ARMS, & LEGS
Make the same as Basic Bear (page 10) then make up in the same way.

Sailor's Trousers

FINISHED SIZE
6¾ in (17 cm) long and 9 in (23 cm) diameter around waist

GAUGE

8 sts and 9 rows measured over 2 in (5 cm) working single crochet in MC and using H-8 (5.00 mm) hook.

FRONT

Foundation row: Using yarn A, beg at front waist edge, make 18ch.

Row 1 (RS): 1dc in 4th ch from hook, 1dc in each ch across, turn (16 dc).

Row 2: 3ch (counts as first dc), miss first dc, 1 dc in each dc across, turn.

Row 3: Join in yarn MC, 1ch, 1sc in each dc across, turn (16 sc).

Row 4: 1ch, 1sc in each sc across.**
Rep last row 10 times more.

Shape left front "V"

Row 15: 1ch, 1sc in each of next 8sc, turn (8 sc).

Row 16: Sl st in first sc, 1ch, 1sc in each of next 7sc, turn (7 sc).

Row 17: 1ch, 1sc in each of next 5sc, skip next sc, 1sc in next sc, turn (6 sc).

Row 18: Sl st in first sc, 1ch, 1sc in each of next 5sc, turn (5 sc).

Row 19: 1ch, 1sc in each of next 3sc, skip next sc, 1sc in next sc, turn (4 sc).

Row 20: Sl st in first sc, 1ch, 1sc in each of next 3sc (3 sc).

Row 21: 1ch, 1sc in each of next 3sc. Fasten off.

Shape right front "V"

Row 15: With RS facing, join in yarn MC to center front, counting in 8sc from side edge, 1ch, 1sc in each of next 8sc, turn (8 sc).

Row 16: 1ch, 1sc in each of next 6sc, skip next sc, 1sc in next sc, turn (7 sc).

Row 17: Sl st in first sc, 1ch, 1sc in each of next 6sc, turn (6 sc).

Row 18: 1ch, 1sc in each of next 4sc, skip next sc, 1sc in next sc, turn (5 sc).

Row 19: Sl st in first sc, 1ch, 1sc in each of next 4sc, turn (4 sc).

Row 20: 1ch, 1sc in each of next 2sc, skip next sc, 1sc in next sc, turn (3 sc).

Row 21: 1ch, 1sc in each of next 3sc. Fasten off.

BACK

Work as for front up to **.
Rep last row 15 times more.

Shape back neck

Next row (WS): 1ch, 1sc in each of next 5sc, turn.

Next row: Sl st in first sc, 1ch, skip next sc, 1sc in each of next 3sc (3 sc). Fasten off.

Next row: With WS facing, skip center 6sc, join in yarn MC to next sc, 1ch, 1sc in same sc, 1sc in each of next 4sc, turn (5 sc).

Next row: 1ch, 1sc in each of next 2sc, skip next sc, 1sc in next sc (3 sc). Fasten off.

Using backstitch, sew up the shoulder seams and, from waist edge 2½ in (6 cm) at each side.

SLEEVES

Make 2 alike.

With RS facing, join in yarn MC in shoulder seam at armhole edge, 1ch, work 23sc evenly around armhole. Place marker, cont working in rnds until sleeve measures 1 in (2.5 cm), ending with sl st in first sc of previous rnd. Fasten off. Weave in ends.

TO FINISH

Weave in all ends.

With RS facing, join in yarn A at lower point of front "V," work in sc evenly around neck edge, sl st to first sc. Fasten off.

BOW FOR SHIRT FRONT

Foundation row: Using yarn B make 19ch.

Row 1: 1sc in 2nd ch from hook, 1sc in each ch across (18 sc).
Fasten off. Weave in ends, twist a loop, sew to front of shirt.

Sailor's Shoes

FINISHED SIZE

2¾ in (7 cm) × 1½ in (4 cm)

MATERIALS

- **RYC** *Cashsoft DK*
  Small amount of Gray 518 (MC)
- Hook: H-8 (5.00 mm)
- Yarn needle

GAUGE

8 sts and 9 rows measured over 2 in
(5 cm) working single crochet in MC and
using H-8 (5.00 mm) hook.

SHOES

Make 2 alike.

Foundation row: Beg at toe, using yarn
MC, make 2ch.

Rnd 1: 6sc in 2nd ch from hook.

Rnd 2: 2sc in each of next 6sc (12 sc).

Rnd 3: 2sc in each of next 12sc (24 sc).

Rnd 4: 1sc in each of next 24sc.

Rep last rnd 4 times more.

Shape top of shoe

Rnd 9: 1ch, (skip next sc, sl st in next sc) 6
times, 1sc in each of next 12sc, turn (18 sts).
Now work in rows.

Shape sides

Next row: 1ch, 1sc in each of next 12sc,
turn.

Rep last row 4 times more.

Fasten off. Sew up the heel seam.

Top of shoe

Join in yarn MC at heel seam, 2ch, work
in hdc evenly around top edge of shoe, sl
st in top of 2ch.

Fasten off. Weave in ends.

Sailor's Cap

FINISHED SIZE

6¾ in (17 cm) diameter

MATERIALS

- **Jaeger** *Roma*
  Small amount of Snow White 001 (A)
- **RYC** *Cashsoft DK*
  Small amount of Gray 518 (B)
- **Anchor** *Tapisserie Wool*
  Small amount of Cherry 8216 for
  hat tassel (C)
- Hook: H-8 (5.00 mm)

GAUGE

8 sts and 9 rows measured over 2 in
(5 cm) working single crochet in MC and
using H-8 (5.00 mm) hook.

CAP

Foundation row: Beg at top, using yarn
A, make 2ch.

Rnd 1: 8sc in 2nd ch from hook.

Rnd 2: *1sc in next sc, 2sc in next sc,
rep from * around (12 sc).

Rnd 3: *1sc in each of next 2sc, 2sc in
next sc, rep from * around (16 sc).

Rnd 4: *1sc in each of next 3sc, 2sc in
next sc, rep from * around (20 sc).

Rnd 5: *1sc in each of next 4sc, 2sc in

next sc, rep from * around (24 sc).

Rnd 6: *1sc in each of next 5sc, 2sc in
next sc, rep from * around (28 sc).

Rnd 7: *1sc in each of next 6sc, 2sc in
next sc, rep from * around (32 sc).

Rnd 8: 1sc in each of next 32sc.

Rep last round twice more.

Rnd 11: *1sc in next sc, skip next sc, rep
from * around (16 sc).

Fasten off.

Rnd 12: Join in yarn B with sl st in last sc,
1ch, 1sc in each of next 16 sc.

Rep last rnd once more. Fasten off.

Rnd 14: Join in yarn MC with sl st in last
sc, 1ch, 1sc in each of next 16sc.

Fasten off. Weave in ends.

TO FINISH

To make the tassel, cut short lengths of
red tapestry yarn, bend in half, and hook
the loop through any sc at the top of the
hat. Pass the raw ends through the loop,
and pull through the loop to lie flat
against the hat. Bunch up the strands,
then tie around the middle with another
length of tapestry yarn. Trim if necessary.
Sew the hat to the bear's head.

Princess Peony

This golden-haired princess will surely win the heart of any little girl. Pretty in pink, she makes an enchanting best friend for any proud owner.

Doll

FINISHED SIZE

16½ in (42 cm) tall × 19¾ in (50 cm) wide (arms outstretched)

MATERIALS

- Jaeger *Aqua Cotton*
  One ball of Talc 302 (MC)
- **Debbie Bliss** *Cashmerino Astrakhan*
  One ball of Gold 0707 for hair (A)
- Hook: E-4 (3.50 mm)
- Small pieces of felt for eyes
- Black thread for sewing on eyes
- Two ¼ in (6 mm) black glass beads or similar for eyes
- Pink embroidery thread for sewing mouth
- Polyester toy fiberfill or batting
- Yarn needle

GAUGE

As for Basic Doll (see page 13).

NOTE:

Before beg the second rnd in each section, place a marker or short length of contrasting yarn across your crochet and up against the loop on the hook and above the working yarn. Work Rnd 2 then slip the marker out and place it at the beg of the next rnd and so on. The marker will indicate where each subsequent rnd starts.

HEAD, BODY, ARMS, FEET, & LEGS

Using yarn MC and E-4 (3.50 mm) hook, make the same as for Basic Doll (see page 13).

Wardrobe

FINISHED SIZE

Gown: 9 in (23 cm) long

MATERIALS

- **Debbie Bliss** *Baby Cashmerino*
  Two balls of Pink 006 (MC)
- **RYC** *Cashsoft 4ply*
  One ball of Rose Lake 421 (A)
- **RYC** *Cashcotton 4ply*
  Small amount of Cyclamen 00911 (B)
- **Karabella Yarns** *Vintage Mercerized Cotton*
  Small amount of Gold 320 (C)
- Hook: E-4 (3.50 mm) and G-6 (4.00 mm)

- Two short lengths of ribbon for top of the hat
- Yarn needle

GAUGE

7 sts and 4½ rnds measured over 2 in (5 cm) working half double crochet in MC and using G-6 (4.00 mm) hook.

GOWN

Foundation row: Beg with bodice, using yarn MC and G-6 (4.00 mm) hook, make 32 ch.

Row 1: 1hdc in 2nd ch from hook, 1hdc in each ch across, join with sl st in first hdc to form ring and cont to work in rnds (31 hdc).

Rnd 1: 1hdc in each of next 31hdc.

Rnd 2: 1hdc in each of next 31hdc.

Rep last rnd 3 times more, ending with sl st in first hdc of rnd. Fasten off yarn MC.

Shape skirt

Rnd 6: Join in yarn A to same place as sl st was worked, 1sc in each of next 15hdc, 3sc in next hdc, 1sc in each of next 15hdc (33 sc).

Rnd 7: 1sc in each of next 15sc, 2sc in next sc, 1sc in each of next 3sc, 2sc in next sc, 1sc in each of next 13sc (35 sc).

Rnd 8: 1sc in each of next 15sc, 2sc in next sc, 1sc in each of next 5sc, 2sc in next sc, 1sc in each of next 13sc (37 sc).

Rnd 9: 1sc in each of next 15sc, 2sc in next sc, 1sc in each of next 7sc, 2sc in next sc, 1sc in each of next 13sc (39 sc).

Rnd 10: 1sc in each of next 15sc, 2sc in next sc, 1sc in each of next 9sc, 2sc in next sc, 1sc in each of next 13sc (41 sc).

Cont increasing at center front until there are 61sc, with 27sc after first increase.

Rnd 20: 1sc in each of next 61sc.

Rep last rnd until gown measures 9 in (23 cm) from top of bodice.

Fasten off.

For the heart motif, make 22ch using yarn C (slipper color) and E-4 (3.50 mm) hook. Fasten off and twist into a heart shape onto the front of the bodice, securing with a few stitches.

RUFFLE

Foundation row: Using yarn B and E-4 (3.50 mm) hook, make 34 ch.

Row 1: 1sc in 2nd ch from hook, 1 sc in each ch across, turn (33 sc).

Row 2: 1ch, 1sc in each sc across, turn (33 sc).

Row 3: 1ch, 1sc in first sc, *skip 1sc, 5dc in next sc, skip 1sc, 1sc in next sc, rep from * to end.

Fasten off.

TO FINISH

Sew the middle three "scallops" of the ruffle onto the center front of the bodice at the foundation row. Join the two ruffle ends, then sew the seam onto the back of the bodice.

PRINCESS HAT

Foundation row: Beg at the pointed top, using yarn B and G-6 (4.00 mm) hook, make 2ch.

Rnd 1: 6sc in 2nd ch from hook.
Rnd 2: 1sc in each of next 6sc (6 sc).
Rnd 3: [1sc in next sc, 2sc in next sc] 3 times (9 sc).
Rnd 4: 1sc in each of next 9sc.
Rnd 5: [1sc in each of next 2sc, 2sc in next sc] 3 times (12 sc).
Rnd 6: 1sc in each of next 12sc.
Rnd 7: [1sc in each of next 3sc, 2sc in next sc] 3 times (15 sc).
Rnd 8: 1sc in each of next 15sc.
Rnd 9: [1sc in each of next 4sc, 2sc in next sc] 3 times (18 sc).
Rnd 10: 1sc in each of next 18sc.
Rnd 11: [1sc in each of next 5sc, 2sc in next sc] 3 times (21 sc).
Rnd 12: [1sc in each of next 6sc, 2sc in next sc] 3 times (24 sc).
Rnd 13: [1sc in each of next 7sc, 2sc in next sc] 3 times (27 sc).
Rnd 14: 1sc in each of next 27sc.
Rnd 15: [1sc in each of next 8sc, 2sc in next sc] 3 times (30 sc).
Rnd 16: 1sc in each of next 30sc.
Rnd 17: [1sc in each of next 9sc, 2sc in next sc] 3 times (33 sc).
Rnd 18: 1sc in each of next 33sc, ending with sl st in top of first sc of rnd. Fasten off.
Join in yarn MC to place where sl st was worked.
Rnd 19: 1hdc in each sc around, ending with sl st in top of first hdc of rnd. Fasten off. Weave in ends. Sew two short lengths of coordinating ribbon to the top of the hat and tie in a bow.
For the chin straps using yarn B, make 2 lengths of 23ch, fasten off and sew to the insides of each side of the hat. Weave in ends.

BELT

Foundation row: Using yarn C and E-4 (3.50 mm) hook, make 42ch.

Row 1: 1sc in 2nd ch from hook, 1sc in each ch across, turn (41 sc).
Row 2: *3ch, sl st in first of these 3ch, skip next sc, 1sc in next sc, repeat from * 16 times more, leaving rem 7sc unworked.
Fasten off.
The remaining few sc are used as the belt end. Tuck this into the first 3ch when belt is placed around waist. Weave in ends.

SLIPPERS

Foundation row: Beg at toe, using yarn C and E-4 (3.50 mm) hook, make 2ch.

Rnd 1: 6sc in 2nd ch from hook.
Rnd 2: 2sc in each of next 6sc (12 sc).
Rnd 3: *1sc in each of next 2sc, 2sc in next sc, rep from * around (16 sc).
Rnd 4: 1sc in each sc around (16 sc).
Rep last rnd twice more.

Shape top of slipper
Rnd 7: (Skip next sc, 1sc in next sc) 4 times, 1sc in each of next 8sc, turn (12 sc).

Shape sides
Now work in rows.
Row 1: 1ch, 1sc in each of next 6sc, turn.
Row 2: 1ch, 2sc in next sc, 1sc in each of next 3sc, 2sc in next sc, 1sc in next sc, turn (8 sc).
Row 3: 1ch, 2sc in next sc, 1sc in each of next 5sc, 2sc in next sc, 1sc in next sc, turn (10 sc).
Row 4: 1ch, 2sc in next sc, 1sc in each of next 7sc, 2sc in next sc, 1sc in next sc, turn (12 sc).
Row 5: 1ch, 1sc in each of next 12sc, turn.
Rep last row twice more.
Fasten off. Sew up the heel seam.

Ankle straps
Make 2 alike.
Make 20ch, fasten off. Weave in ends. Join the center of the strap to the heel seam. Tie straps onto foot.

Molly the Mermaid

Elegant and serene, Molly's flowing locks and beautiful blue eyes make her a sight to behold at sea or on land. Join her in her underwater palace and watch the hours float by.

Mermaid

FINISHED SIZE

16 in (41 cm) tall × 19¾ in (50 cm) wide (arms outstretched)

MATERIALS

- **Jaeger *Pure Cotton DK***
  One ball of Shell 0576 (MC)
- **Rowan *All Seasons Cotton***
  One ball of Lime Leaf 217 for tail (A)
- **Sirdar *Breeze***
  Small amount of Lime 068 for
  tail fins (B)
- **Anchor *Tapisserie Wool***
  Small amount of 9096 and 9156 for
  tail ruffles in order of making (C)
- **Rowan *4ply Cotton***
  Small amount of 120 Orchid for shell
  in hair and for mouth (D)
- **Brown Sheep Company *Cotton Fleece***
  One ball of Banana 620 for hair (E)
- Hook: E-4 (3.50 mm) and C-2 (2.50 mm)
- Small pieces of felt for eyes
- Black and pink embroidery thread for sewing on eyes and mouth detail
- Two ¼ in (6 mm) black glass beads or similar for eyes
- Polyester toy fiberfill or batting
- Yarn needle

GAUGE

12 sts and 12 rnds measured over 2 in (5 cm) working single crochet in MC and using E-4 (3.50 mm) hook.

NOTE:

Before beg the second rnd in each section, place a marker or short length of contrasting yarn across your crochet and up against the loop on the hook and above the working yarn. Work Rnd 2 then slip the marker out and place it at the beg of the next rnd and so on. The marker will indicate where each subsequent rnd starts.

HEAD, BODY, & ARMS

Using yarn MC and E-4 (3.50 mm) hook, make the same as for Basic Doll (page 13).

NOTE:

For the mermaid, make only the trunk of the Basic Doll.

TAIL

Foundation rnd: Using yarn A and E-4 (3.50 mm) hook, beg at the tip of the tail, make 3ch, join with a sl st to form ring.

Rnd 1: Working over tail end, 1sc in next ch, 2sc in next ch, 1sc in last ch (4 sc).

Rnd 2: 1sc in each of next 4sc.

Rnd 3: 2sc in each of next 4sc (8 sc).

Rnd 4: 1sc in each of next 8sc.

Rep last rnd once more.

Rnd 6: 1sc in next sc, 2sc in next sc, 1sc in each of next 3sc, 2sc in next sc, 1sc in each of next 2sc (10 sc).

Rnd 7: 1sc in each of next 10sc.

Rep last rnd once more.

Rnd 9: [1sc in each of next 2sc, 2sc in next sc] 3 times, 1sc in next sc (13 sc).

Rnd 10: 1sc in each of next 13sc.

Rep last rnd once more.

Rnd 12: [1sc in each of next 3sc, 2sc in next sc] 3 times, 1sc in next sc (16 sc).

Rnd 13: 1sc in each of next 16sc.

Rep last rnd once more.

Rnd 15: [1sc in each of next 7sc, 2sc in next sc] twice (18 sc).

Rnd 16: 1sc in each of next 18sc.

Rep last rnd once more.

Rnd 18: [1sc in each of next 8sc, 2sc in next sc] twice (20 sc).

Rnd 19: 1sc in each of next 20sc.

Rep last rnd once more.

Rnd 21: 1ch, 1sc in each of next 20sc, turn (21 sts).

Shell pattern

Row 1: 4ch, 3tr in first sc, [skip 3sc, 1sc in next sc, skip 3sc, 7tr in next sc] twice, skip 3sc, 1sc in 1ch at beg of previous row, turn.

Row 2: 4ch, 3tr in first sc, [skip 3tr, 1sc in next tr (the center tr of 7), skip 3tr, 7tr in next sc] twice, skip 3tr, 1sc in 4th of 4ch at beg of previous row, turn.
Rep last row 5 times more.
Fasten off.

TAIL RUFFLE

Make 4 ruffles—one in yarn A, one in yarn B and 2 in the other yarn C.

Foundation row: Using appropriate yarn and using E-4 (3.50 mm) hook, make 30ch.

Row 1: 1sc in 2nd ch from hook, 1sc in each ch across, turn (29 sc).

Row 2: 1ch, 1sc in each sc across (29 sc).

Row 3: 1ch, 1sc in first sc, *skip 1sc, 5dc in next sc, skip 1sc, 1sc in next sc, rep from * to end.
Fasten off.

TAIL FINS

Make 2 alike.

Foundation rnd: Using yarn B and E-4 (3.50 mm) hook, beg at the tip of the tail, make 4ch, join with a sl st to form ring.

Rnd 1: Working over tail end, [1sc in next ch, 2sc in next ch] twice (6 sc).

Rnd 2: 1sc in each of next 6sc.

Rnd 3: [1sc in next sc, 2sc in next sc] 3 times (9 sc).

Rnd 4: 1sc in each of next 9sc.

Rnd 5: [1sc in next sc, 2sc in next sc] 4 times, 1sc in next sc (13 sc).

Rnd 6: 1sc in each sc around.

Rnd 7: [1sc in next sc, 2sc in next sc] 6 times, 1sc in next sc (19 sc).

Rnd 8: 1 sc in each of next 19sc.
Rep last rnd 5 times more.

Rnd 14: [1sc in each of next 2sc, skip next sc] 6 times, 1sc in next sc (13 sc).

Rnd 15: 1sc in each of next 13sc.

Rnd 16: [1sc in next sc, skip next sc] 6 times, 1sc in next sc (7 sc).

Rnd 17: 1sc in each of next 7sc.
Rep last rnd once more.
Fasten off.

SHELL (IN HAIR)

Foundation row: Using yarn D and C-2 (2.50 mm) hook, make 6ch.

Row 1: 1sc in 2nd ch from hook, 1 sc in each ch across (5 sc).

Row 2: 1ch, 1sc in each sc across (5 sc).

Row 3: 1ch, 1sc in first sc, skip 1sc, 5dc in next sc, skip 1sc, 1sc in next sc.
Fasten off.

TO FINISH

Follow instructions for Basic Doll (page 13).

Sew the finishing row of the first tail ruffle to the top of the tail (the wavy edges should lie over the top of the tail). Sew up the tail along the back seam. Ease to fit the top of the tail to the bottom edge of the body, over-sew in place. Sew on the other three ruffles so that they fall one-third of the way down the tail.

At the tip of the tail, over-sew the two tail fins at either side of the tail.

To sew on hair, cut yarn E into lengths of 14¼ in (36 cm) and follow instructions for Basic Doll (page 13). Sew the hair shell in place at the side of the head.

Tankini

MATERIALS

- **RYC *Cashsoft DK***
  Small amount of Ballad Blue 508 (MC)
- **Sirdar *Breeze***
  Small amount of Wisteria 069 for ruffle (A)
- Hook: E-4 (3.50 mm)
- Yarn needle

BACK AND FRONT

Foundation row: Using yarn A, beg with

the ruffle, make 50ch.

Row 1: 1sc in 2nd ch from hook, 1sc in next ch, *3ch, skip 1ch, 1sc in each of next 3ch, rep from * to last 3ch, 3ch, skip 1ch, 1sc in each of last 2ch, turn.

Row 2: 1ch, 1sc in first sc, *skip 1sc, 5dc in next 3ch loop, skip 1sc, 1sc in next sc, rep from * to end, turn.

Row 3: 5ch, skip first sc and next dc, *1sc in each of next 3dc, 3ch, skip (1dc, 1sc and 1dc), rep from * to last 5dc group, 1sc in each of next 3dc, 2ch, skip 1dc, 1dc in last sc.

Fasten off.

With RS facing, join in yarn MC to corner of foundation row edge and work 34sc evenly across straight edge of ruffle, turn.

Next row: 1ch, 1sc in each of next 34sc, turn.

Rep last row once more.

Fasten off.

STRAPS

Make 2 alike.

In yarn MC, make 12ch.

Fasten off.

TO FINISH

Sew up the back seam, oversew the straps at the arm positions. Fit the top onto the mermaid for accurate positioning.

Mirror

MATERIALS

- **Opal *Uni 4ply***
  Small amount of Hot Pink 1413 for back and handle (MC)
- **Rowan *Lurex Shimmer***
  Small amount of Pewter 333 for glass (A)
- Hook size: C-2 (2.50 mm)
- Yarn needle

MIRROR BACK

Foundation row: Using yarn MC, make 2ch.

**Rnd 1: 6sc in 2nd ch from hook, join with sl st to first sc to form ring (6 sc).

Rnd 2: 1sc in each of next 6sc.

Rnd 3: [1sc in next sc, 2sc in next sc] 3 times (9 sc).**

Rnd 4: 2sc in each of next 9sc, sl st in first sc of rnd (18 sc).

Handle

Make 10 ch.

Row 1: 1dc in 4th ch from hook, 1dc in each of next 4ch, 1hdc in next ch, [1sc, 1ch, 1sc] in last ch.

Fasten off. Weave in ends to stabilize handle.

MIRROR GLASS

Foundation row: Using yarn A, make 2ch.

Work as for Mirror Back from ** to **.

Fasten off.

Sew the glass to the mirror back. Sew the mirror handle to the mermaid's right hand.

Animal Kingdom

These projects come to life with a little imagination and make excellent presents for boys and girls of all ages! Join Larry the Lobster in his hunt for some freshwater fun or drift off to sleep with Sir Waldorf Walrus on his afternoon nap—or maybe joining Jenna the Giraffe at her afternoon tea party is more your scene?

George the Shark

Don't let his beady eyes and powerful tail deceive you. With embroidered facial features, a floppy fin, and a big, white belly, George is the cutest creature in the big blue sea and a loving companion for your small fry.

Shark

FINISHED SIZE

13½ in (34 cm) long

MATERIALS

- **RYC Cashsoft Aran**
  One ball of Tornado 008 (MC)
- **Debbie Bliss Cashmerino Aran**
  One ball of Cream 300101 for belly (A)
- Hook: K-10½ (6.50 mm) and H-8 (5.00 mm)
- Thread for attaching beads
- Black DK (light worsted weight) yarn for mouth
- Two ¼ in (6 mm) black glass beads or similar for eyes
- Polyester toy fiberfill or batting
- Yarn needle

GAUGE

7 sts and 6½ rows measured over 2 in (5 cm) working in single crochet in yarn MC and using and K-10½ (6.50 mm) hook.

NOTE:

Before beg the second rnd in each section, place a marker or short length of contrasting yarn across your crochet and up against the loop on the hook and above the working yarn. Work Rnd 2 then slip the marker out and place it at the beg of the next rnd and so on. The marker will indicate where each subsequent rnd starts.

BODY

Foundation row: Beg at the nose, in yarn MC and using K-10½ (6.50 mm) hook, make 2ch.
Rnd 1: 6sc in 2nd ch from hook.
Rnd 2: 1sc in each of next 6sc.
Rep last rnd once more.
Rnd 4: *1sc in next sc, 2sc in next sc, rep from * around (9 sc).
Rnd 5: 1sc in each of next 9sc.
Rep last rnd once more.
Rnd 7: *1sc in each of next 2sc, 2sc in next sc, rep from * around (12 sc).
Rnd 8: 1sc in each of next 12sc.
Now work back section by cont to work in rows.
Row 1: 1ch, 1sc in each of next 10sc, turn.
Row 2: 2ch, 1sc in 2nd ch from hook, 1sc in each of next 9sc, 2sc in last sc, turn (12 sc).
Row 3: 1ch, 1sc in each of next 12sc across, turn.

Rep last row 7 times more.
Row 11: 2ch, 1sc in 2nd ch from hook, 1sc in each sc to last sc, 2sc in last sc, turn (14 sc).
Row 12: 1sc in each sc across, turn.
Rep last 2 rows twice more (18 sc).
Row 17: 1sc in each sc across, turn.
Rep last row 6 times more.
Row 24: Place marker here, sl st in first sc, 1ch, 1sc in each of next 15sc, skip next sc, 1sc in last sc, place marker here, turn (16 sc).
Row 25: Sl st in first sc, 1ch, 1sc in each of next 13sc, skip next sc, 1sc in last sc, turn (14 sc).
Row 26: 1ch, 1sc in each sc across, turn.
Rep last row once more.
Row 28: Sl st in first sc, 1ch, 1sc in each of next 11sc, skip next sc, 1sc in last sc, turn (12 sc).
Row 29: 1ch, 1sc in each sc across, turn.
Rep last row 4 times more.
Row 34: Sl st in first sc, 1ch, 1sc in each of next 9sc, skip next sc, 1sc in last sc, join with sl st in first sl st of row to form a ring (10 sc).
Shape tail
Rnd 1: 1sc in each of next 10sc around.
Rnd 2: [2sc in next sc, 1sc in each of next 4sc] twice (12 sc).

Rnd 3: [2sc in next sc, 1sc in each of next 5sc] twice (14 sc).

Rnd 4: [2sc in next sc, 1sc in each of next 6sc] twice (16 sc).

Rnd 5: [2sc in next sc, 1sc in each of next 7sc] twice (18 sc).

Rnd 6: 1sc in each sc around (18 sc).

Shape bottom of tail

Rnd 7: 1sc in each of next 3sc, place marker here, turn.

Now cont to work in rows to shape bottom tail.

Row 1: 1ch, 1sc in each of next 6sc, turn. Rep last row once more.

Row 3: Sl st in first sc, 1ch, 1sc in each of next 3sc, skip next sc, 1sc in last sc, turn (4 sc).

Row 4: 1ch, 1sc in each of next 4sc, turn.

Row 5: Sl st in first sc, 1ch, 1sc in next sc, skip next sc, 1sc in last sc (2 sc).

Fasten off, leaving a tail end for sewing up with later.

Top tail

Join in yarn MC with sl st in sc at marker on Rnd 7 of "Shape bottom of tail."

Row 1: 1ch, 1sc in each of next 13sc, turn.

Rep last row twice more.

Row 4: Sl st in first sc, 1ch, 1sc in each of next 10sc, skip next sc, 1sc in last sc, turn (11 sc).

Row 5: Sl st in first sc, 1ch, 1sc in each of next 8sc, skip next sc, 1sc in last sc, turn (9 sc).

Row 6: Sl st in first sc, 1ch, 1sc in each of next 6sc, skip next sc, 1sc in last sc, turn (7 sc).

Row 7: Sl st in first sc, 1ch, 1sc in each of next 4sc, skip next sc, 1sc in last sc, turn (5 sc).

Row 8: Sl st in first sc, 1ch, 1sc in each of next 2sc, skip next sc, 1sc in last sc, turn (3 sc).

Row 9: Skip first 2 sc, sl st in last sc. Fasten off and weave in the loose end.

BELLY

Foundation row: Beg at the chin, in yarn A and using K-10½ (6.50 mm) hook, make 7ch.

Row 1: 1sc in 2nd ch from hook, 1sc in each ch across, turn (6 sc).

Row 2: 2ch, 1sc in 2nd ch from hook, 1sc in each sc to last sc, 2sc in last sc, turn (8 sc).

Rep last row twice more (12 sc).

Row 5: 1ch, 1sc in each sc across, turn. Rep last row twice more.

Row 8: 2ch, 1sc in 2nd ch from hook, 1sc in each sc to last sc, 2sc in last sc, turn (14 sc).

Row 9: 1ch, 1sc in each sc across, turn. Rep last row once more.

Row 11: Sl st in first sc, 1ch, 1sc in each of next 11sc, skip next sc, 1sc in last sc, turn (12 sc).

Row 12: 1ch, 1sc in each sc across, turn. Rep last row once more.

Row 14: Sl st in first sc, 1ch, 1sc in each of next 9sc, skip next sc, 1sc in last sc, turn (10 sc).

Row 15: 1ch, 1sc in each sc across, turn. Rep last row once more.

Row 17: Sl st in first sc, 1ch, 1sc in each of next 7sc, skip next sc, 1sc in last sc, turn (8 sc).

Row 18: 1ch, 1sc in each sc across, turn. Rep last row once more.

Row 20: Sl st in first sc, 1ch, 1sc in each of next 5sc, skip next sc, 1sc in last sc, turn (6 sc).

Row 21: 1ch, 1sc in each sc across, turn.

Row 22: Sl st in first sc, 1ch, 1sc in each of next 3sc, skip next sc, 1sc in last sc, turn (4 sc).

Row 23: Sl st in first sc, 1ch, 1sc in next sc, skip next sc, 1sc in last sc, turn (2 sc).

Row 24: Skip first sc, sl st in last sc. Fasten off.

DORSAL FIN

Foundation row: Beg at the pointed top, in yarn MC and using H-8 (5.00 mm) hook, make 2ch.

Rnd 1: 4sc in 2nd ch from hook.

Rnd 2: 1sc in each of next 4sc.

Rnd 3: 1sc in each of next 3sc, 2sc in next sc (5 sc).

Rnd 4: 1sc in each of next 4sc, 2sc in next sc (6 sc).

Rnd 5: 1sc in each of next 5sc, 2sc in next sc (7 sc).

Rnd 6: 1sc in each of next 6sc, 2sc in next sc (8 sc).

Rnd 7: 1sc in each of next 7sc, 2sc in next sc (9 sc).

Cont increasing 1sc on last sc of rnd for 4 more rnds (13 sc).

Fasten off, leaving a tail end for sewing to body later.

UPPER TAIL FIN

Foundation row: Beg at the pointed top, in yarn MC and using H-8 (5.00 mm) hook, make 2ch.

Rnd 1: 4sc in 2nd ch from hook.

Rnd 2: 1sc in each of next 4sc.

Rnd 3: 1sc in each of next 3sc, 2sc in next sc (5 sc).

Rnd 4: 1sc in each of next 4sc, 2sc in next sc (6 sc).

Rnd 5: 1sc in each of next 5sc, 2sc in next sc (7 sc).

Fasten off, leaving a tail end for sewing up to the body later.

LOWER TAIL FIN

Foundation row: Beg at the pointed top, in yarn MC and using H-8 (5.00 mm) hook, make 2ch.

Rnd 1: 4sc in 2nd ch from hook.

Rnd 2: 1sc in each of next 4sc.

Rnd 3: 1sc in each of next 3sc, 2sc in next sc (5 sc).

Rnd 4: 1sc in each of next 4sc, 2sc in next sc (6 sc).

Rnd 5: 1sc in each of next 5sc, 2sc in next sc (7 sc).

Rnd 6: 1sc in each of next 6sc, 2sc in next sc (8 sc).

Rnd 7: 1sc in each of next 7sc, 2sc in next sc (9 sc).

Fasten off, leaving a tail end for sewing up to the body later.

FRONT FINS

Make 4—2 using yarn MC and 2 using yarn A.

Foundation row: Using K-10½ (6.50 mm) hook, beg at the end which is sewn to the body, make 5ch.

Row 1: 1sc in 2nd ch from hook, 1sc in each of next 2ch, 2sc in last ch, turn (5 sc).

Row 2: 2ch, 1sc in 2nd ch from hook, 1sc in each sc across, turn (6 sc).

Row 3: 1ch, 1sc in each sc to last sc, 2sc in last sc, turn (7 sc).

Row 4: Sl st in first sc, 1ch, 1sc in each sc across, turn (6 sc).

Row 5: 1ch, 1sc in each sc across to last 2sc, skip next sc, 1sc in last sc, turn (5 sc). Rep last 2 rows once more (3 sc).

Row 8: Skip first 2 sc, sl st in last sc, turn, make 1ch, and work in sc evenly all around the edge of the fin, sl st to first sc. Fasten off and weave in the end.

TO FINISH

With RS facing and working backstitch, sew up bottom tail fin along the decreases, sew up the top tail fin.

Sew the belly to the chin and along the body to first markers, leaving a gap for turning through and stuffing. Stuff and close the gap. Turn RS out.

Mold the tail fins into a point with your fingers, weave in the ends at the pointed ends, use the other ends to sew the larger fin under the body just before the tail begins and the upper fin to the top of the body just before the tail.

Sew the dorsal fin halfway along the body to the upper edge. Weave in the end at the point and shape if necessary.

Sew up the under body, up to the first set of markers.

Make 2 sets of front fins by sewing one fin in MC to one fin in yarn A around the edges. Sew front fins to sides of body where body meets belly, referring to photograph for positioning.

Sew on two beads for eyes 2 in (5 cm) from point of nose and spaced 2 in (5 cm) apart. Sew a mouth using the the black yarn, curving the mouth around the nose where the body meets the belly, starting and ending in line with the eyes and working a row of stem stitch.

Kangaroo Bag with Joey

Fill your 'roo's stomach with supplies from the Outback! Totally practical yet fun and huggable, this double-crocheted carryall has a drawstring closure, durable straps (shaped as the ears), and ample space to keep all your young one's belongings. A cutesy joey fits comfortably and cozily in the front pouch.

Kangaroo Bag

FINISHED SIZE

Approximately 15 in (38 cm) long × 14¼ in (36 cm) at widest point

MATERIALS

- **Jaeger** *Natural Fleece* Two balls of Cameo 521 (MC)
- **Rowan** *Big Wool* Two balls of Cream 01 for tummy (A)
- **Debbie Bliss** *Cashmerino Aran* Two balls of Brown 300105 for nose and eyes (B)
- Hook: N-15 (10.00 mm) and H-8 (5.00 mm)
- Yarn needle

GAUGE

5 sts and 5 rows measured over 2 in (5 cm) working in single crochet in yarn MC and using N-15 (10.00 mm) hook.

NOTE:

Before beg the second rnd in each section, place a marker or short length of contrasting yarn across your crochet and up against the loop on the hook and above the working yarn. Work Rnd 2 then slip the marker out and place it at the beg of the next rnd and so on. The marker will indicate where each subsequent rnd starts.

BAG

Foundation row: Using yarn MC and N-15 (10.00 mm) hook, beg at the round base, make 2ch.

Rnd 1: 6sc in 2nd ch from hook.

Rnd 2: 2sc in each of next 6sc (12 sc).

Rnd 3: *1sc in next sc, 2sc in next sc, rep from * around (18 sc).

Rnd 4: *1sc in each of next 2sc, 2sc in next sc, rep from * around (24 sc).

Rnd 5: *1sc in each of next 3sc, 2sc in next sc, rep from * around (30 sc).

Rnd 6: *1sc in each of next 4sc, 2sc in next sc, rep from * around (36 sc).

Rnd 7: *1sc in each of next 5sc, 2sc in next sc, rep from * around (42 sc).

Cont working in this patt for 5 rnds more, inc 1sc in each rep before the 2sc, until you have worked one rnd with 10sc, then 2 in each rep (72 sc).

Shape sides

Rnd 13: 1sc in each of next 72sc.

Rep last round 4 times more.

Shape back

Row 1: 1ch, 1sc in each of next 40sc, turn.

Rep last row 7 times more.

Row 9: 1ch, *1sc in each of next 7sc, skip next sc, rep from * to end, turn (35 sc).

Row 10: 1ch, 1sc in each of next 35sc, turn.

Rep last row 7 times more.

Row 18: 1ch, *1sc in each of next 6sc, skip next sc, rep from * to end, turn (30 sc).

Row 19: 1ch, 1sc in each of next 30sc, turn.

Rep last row 7 times more.

Shape head flap

Row 27: 1ch, 1sc in each of next 22sc, turn.

Row 28: 1ch, 1sc in each of next 14sc, turn.

Rep last row once more.

Row 30: Sl st next sc, 1ch, 1sc in each sc to last 2 sc, skip next sc, 1sc in last sc, turn (12 sc).

Row 31: 1ch, 1sc in each sc across.

Rep last 2 rows 3 times more (6 sc).

Row 38: 1ch, 1sc in each of next 6sc, turn.

Rep last row twice more.

Make nose

Fasten off yarn MC, join in yarn B.

Rep last row 3 times more. Fasten off.

Shape front

With RS facing, join on yarn A with sl st in first sc of rem 32 sc left around last rnd of base.

Row 1: 1ch, 1sc in each of next 32 sc, turn.

Rep last row 7 times more.

Row 9: 1ch, *1sc in each of next 7sc, skip next sc, rep from * to end, turn (28 sts).

Row 10: 1ch, 1sc in each of next 28sc, turn.

Rep last row 7 times more.

Row 18: 1ch, *1sc in each of next 6sc, skip next sc, rep from * to end, turn (24 sts).

Row 19: 1ch, 1sc in each of next 24sc, turn.

Rep last row 7 times more.

Fasten off.

each of 12sc at center of the front of the bag, turn.

Row 1: 1ch, 1sc in each of next 12sc, turn.

Rep last row 8 times more.

Fasten off, leaving a long tail end for sewing up the sides onto the front of the bag.

EARS

Make 2 alike.

Foundation row: Beg at the bottom of the ear—the end that is sewn onto the head. Using yarn A and N-15 (10.00 mm) hook and leaving a long tail end to sew onto the outer ear, make 10ch.

Row 1: 1dc in 4th ch from hook, 1dc in each of next 4ch, 1hdc in next ch, [1sc, 1ch, 1sc] in last ch, cont along lower edge of ch, 1hdc between hdc and next dc, [1dc between next 2dc] 4 times, 1dc between last dc and 3ch at beg of row.

NOTE: *Do not fasten off.*

Border

Next rnd: 1ch, work in sc evenly around outer edge of ear, sl st to 1st sc.

Fasten off.

STRAPS

Make 2 alike.

Foundation row: Using yarn A and N-15 (10.00 mm) hook, make 34ch.

Row 1: 1sc in 2nd ch from hook, 1sc in

each ch to end, turn (33 sc).

Row 2: 1ch, 1sc in each sc to end, turn.

Rep last row once more. Fasten off leaving a long tail end for sewing on the straps.

TO FINISH

With RS facing and using yarn B and satin stitch, sew an eye to each side of the top of the head flap. Sew on the straps at the back of the bag, placing the tops of the straps 2sc apart at the center of the back of the back just under the drawstring, then sew the other ends of the straps at the base of the bag where "shape sides" begins and where yarn MC joins yarn A. Sew the base of the ears at the top of the head flap—7sc apart, then sew the tip of the ears onto the strap, so that when the bag straps are held up the ears are held up, too.

Joey

FINISHED SIZE

Approximately 5 in (13 cm) tall

MATERIALS

- **Rooster *Almerino DK***
  One ball of Hazelnut 202 (MC)
  One ball of Cornish 201 (A)
- **Debbie Bliss *Cashmerino Aran***
  Small amount of Baby pink 603
  for inner ear (B)

DRAWSTRING

Using yarn A and N-15 (10.00 mm) hook, make 100ch, fasten off. Weave in ends. Use this drawstring to weave in and out in every other sc along the top edge, both ends emerging at the center front of bag.

POUCH

Foundation row: At the front of the bag at the point where yarn A joins yarn MC, on the next sc row join in yarn A and using N-15 (10.00 mm) hook, work 1sc in

- Hook: H-8 (5.00 mm)
- Brown yarn or embroidery thread for eyes and nose
- Polyester toy fiberfill or batting
- Yarn needle

GAUGE

8 sts and 7 rows measured over 2 in (5 cm) working in single crochet in yarn MC and using H-8 (5.00 mm) hook.

HEAD

Foundation row: Beg at the nose, using yarn MC and H-8 (5.00 mm) hook, make 2ch.

Rnd 1: 6sc in 2nd ch from hook.

Rnd 2: 1sc in each sc around.

Rep last round twice more.

Rnd 5: *1sc in next sc, 2sc in next sc, rep from * around (9 sc).

Rnd 6: 1sc in each sc around.

Rnd 7: *1sc in each of next 2sc, 2sc in next sc, rep from * around (12 sc).

Rnd 8: 1sc in each sc around.

Rep last round twice more.

Rnd 11: *1sc in each of next 2sc, skip next sc, rep from * around (8 sc).

Stuff the head. Weave in end at the nose.

Rnd 12: *1sc in each next 2sc, skip next sc, rep from * until the round is closed. Fasten off and weave in end.

INNER EARS

Make 2 alike.

Foundation row: Beg at the bottom of the ear—the end that is sewn nearest to the head. Using yarn B, and leaving a long tail end for sewing onto the outer ear, make 10ch.

Row 1: 1dc in 4th ch from hook, 1dc in each of next 4ch, 1hdc in next ch, [1sc, 1ch, 1sc] in last ch, cont along lower edge of ch, 1hdc between hdc and next dc, [1dc between next 2dc] 4 times, 1dc between last dc and 3ch at beg of row. Fasten off, weave in end.

OUTER EARS

Make 2 alike.

Foundation row: Beg at the bottom of the ear—the end that is sewn nearest to the head. Using yarn MC, and leaving a long tail end for sewing onto the head, make 10ch.

Work as for inner ear from ** to **.

NOTE: *Do not fasten off.*

Border

Next rnd: 1ch, work in sc evenly around outer edge of ear, sl st to 1st sc. Fasten off, weave in end.

BODY

Foundation row: Beg at the bottom, using yarn MC, make 2ch.

Rnd 1: 6sc in 2nd ch from hook.

Rnd 2: 2sc in each of next 6sc (12 sc).

Rnd 3: 2sc in each of next 12sc (24 sc).

Rnd 4: 1sc in each sc around.

Rep last round 5 times more.

Shape back

Row 1: 1ch, 1sc in each of next 16sc, place marker, turn (16 sc).

Rep last row once more.

Row 3: 1ch, *skip next sc, 1sc in each of next 3 sc, rep from * across, turn (12 sc).

Row 4: 1ch, 1sc in each sc across, turn (12 sc).

Row 5: 1ch, *skip next sc, 1sc in each of next 2sc, rep from * across, turn (8 sc).

Row 6: 1ch, 1sc in each sc across, turn (8 sc).

Rep last row once more, fasten off.

Shape front

Row 1: Join in yarn A to sc at 1st marker, 1ch, 1sc in each of rem 8 sc at front, 1sc in next sc, turn (9 sc).

Row 2: 1ch, 1sc in each sc across, turn.

Row 3: 1ch, *skip next sc, 1sc in each of next 2sc, rep from * across, turn (6 sc).

Row 4: 1ch, 1sc in each sc across, turn (12 sc).

Row 5: 1ch, *skip next sc, 1sc in next sc, rep from * across, turn (3 sc).

Row 6: 1ch, 1sc in each sc across, turn (3 sc).

Rep last row once more, fasten off.

Sew up the row ends to join front to back, leaving the neck edges open.

Turn RS out.

Shape top

Rnd 1: Join in yarn MC with sl st in any sc at neck edge, 1ch, 1sc in each sc around (11 sc).

Rnd 2: 1sc in each of next 11sc.

Rep last rnd once more.

Rnd 4: 1sc in next sc, [skip next sc, 1sc in next sc] 5 times (6 sc).

Stuff the body.

Rnd 5: *1sc in each of next 2sc, skip next sc, rep from * until the rnd is closed.

Fasten off leaving a long tail end—use this to sew the body to the head.

HIND LEGS

Make 2 alike.

Foundation row: Beg at toe, using yarn MC, make 2ch.

Rnd 1: 6sc in 2nd ch from hook.

Rnd 2: *1sc in next sc, 2sc in next sc, rep from * around (9 sc).

Rnd 3: 1sc in each sc around.

Rep last round 8 times more.

Shape heel

Row 1: 1sc in each of next 4sc, turn.

Row 2: 1ch, 1sc in each of next 4sc, turn.

Rep last round once more.

Fasten off. Join heel seam—fold the finishing row (last 4sc) in half so that the 2 ends meet and sew together to form back of heel.

Shape leg

Rnd 1: Join in yarn MC with a sl st at top of heel seam, 4sc along 1st row-end edge of heel, 1sc in each of 5sc across front of foot, then 4sc along 2nd row-end edge of heel (13 sc).

Stuff foot lightly.

Rnd 2: 1sc in each of next 13sc.

Rep last round 5 times more.

Rnd 8: *1sc in next sc, skip next sc, rep from * until the round is closed.

Fasten off, leaving a long loose end for sewing onto body.

ARMS

Make 2 alike.

Foundation row: Using yarn MC make 6ch.

Row 1: 1sc in 2nd ch from hook, 1sc in each of next 4ch, make 4 ch (9 sts).

Fasten off. Weave in ends, leaving a tail end for sewing to the body.

TAIL

Foundation row: Beg at body end, using yarn MC, make 2ch.

Rnd 1: 6sc in 2nd ch from hook.

Rnd 2: *1sc in next sc, 2sc in next sc, rep from * around (9 sc).

Rnd 3: 1sc in each sc around.

Rep last rnd 9 times more.

Rnd 13: *1sc in each of next 2sc, skip next sc, rep from * around (6 sc).

Rep last rnd 4 times more.

Rnd 18: *1sc in next sc, skip next sc, rep from * until the rnd is closed.

Fasten off. Weave in end.

TO FINISH

Using matching yarn, sew each inner ear to the outer ears, matching top to top and bottom to bottom. Sew each ear to the back of the head.

With the toe end facing towards the front, sew one side of each leg to the body—refer to the photograph for actual placing.

Sew each arm to the front of the body at the top of the front shaping.

Sew the tail to the back of the body.

Using brown yarn or embroidery thread, stitch a French knot for an eye on each side of the head. Sew a row of straight satin stitches close together for the nose.

Jenna the Giraffe

With her snazzy striped dress and fanciful scarf, Jenna's a gentle giant with a sweet tooth. This fun and whimsical giraffe boasts plenty of attitude and bold style. Subtle details—including her flirty embroidered eyelashes, spots along her neck, and a gingham bow around her horn—lend a bounty of personality and character.

Giraffe

FINISHED SIZE
19¼ in (49 cm) tall × 21¾ in (55 cm) with forelegs outstretched

MATERIALS
- **Jaeger *Roma***
  One ball of Orange 008 (MC)
  One ball of Brown 012 (A)
- **Artesano *Alpaca***
  Small amount of Inca Cloud 002 for hooves and mane (B)
- Hook: H-8 (5.00 mm) and G-6 (4.00 mm)
- Pink and brown embroidery thread or fine yarn for mouth and nose
- Two ¼ in (6 mm) black glass beads or similar for eyes
- Black thread for eyelashes
- 12 in (30 cm) × ¼ in (6 mm) ribbon
- Polyester toy fiberfill or batting
- Yarn needle

GAUGE
9 sts and 8 rnds measured over 2 in (5 cm) working single crochet in MC and using H-8 (5.00 mm) hook.

NOTE:
Before beg the second rnd in each section, place a marker or short length of contrasting yarn across your crochet and up against the loop on the hook and above the working yarn. Work Rnd 2 then slip the marker out and place it at the beg of the next rnd and so on. The marker will indicate where each subsequent rnd starts.

HEAD AND BODY
Foundation row: Beg at the nose, using yarn MC and H-8 (5.00 mm) hook, make 2ch.
Rnd 1: 6sc in 2nd ch from hook.
Rnd 2: [1sc in next sc, 2sc in next sc] 3 times (9 sc).
Rnd 3: 1sc in each of next 9sc.
Rep last rnd twice more.
Shape head
Rnd 6: [1sc in each of next 2sc, 2sc in next sc] 3 times (12 sc).
Rnd 7: 2sc in each of next 12sc (24 sc).
Rnd 8: 1sc in each of next 24sc.
Rep last rnd twice more.
Shape back of head
Rnd 11: *1sc in each of next 2sc, skip next

sc, rep from * around (16 sc).
Rnd 12: *1sc in next sc, skip next sc, rep from * around (8 sc).
Shape top of neck
Row 1: 1ch, 1sc in each of next 4sc, turn.
Rep last row once more, ending sl st in next sc.
Fasten off. Sew up finishing row at back of neck by folding last 4sc in half and sewing together.
Stuff the head, avoiding the tip of the nose. Flatten the tip of the nose with your finger and use the tail end at the foundation row to sew up the end with a few stitches. Weave in the end.
Shape neck
Rnd 1: Join on yarn MC with a sl st in a sc near seam, 1sc in each sc and row-end edge around neck, join into ring with sl st in first sc of rnd (9 sc).
Rnd 2: 1sc in each of next 9sc.
Rep last rnd 10 times more, stuffing the neck as you crochet.
Rnd 13: 1sc in each of next 4sc, 2sc in next sc, 1sc in each of next 4sc (10 sc).
Rnd 14: 1sc in each of next 10sc.
Rep last rnd twice more.
Rnd 17: 1sc in each of next 4sc, 2sc in

each of next 2sc, 1sc in each of next 4sc (12 sc).

Rnd 18: 1sc in each of next 12sc.
Rep last rnd twice more.

Rnd 21: 1sc in each of next 4sc, 2sc in each of next 4sc, 1sc in each of next 4sc (16 sc).

Shape body

Rnd 22: *1sc in next sc, 2sc in next sc, rep from * around (24 sc).

Rnd 23: *1sc in each of next 2sc, 2sc in next sc, rep from * around (32 sc).

Rnd 24: 1sc in each of next 32sc.
Rep last rnd 9 times more.

Shape bottom

Rnd 34: *1sc in each of next 7sc, skip next sc, rep from * around (28 sc).

Rnd 35: 1sc in each of next 28sc.

Rnd 36: *1sc in each of next 6sc, skip next sc, rep from * around (24 sc).

Rnd 37: 1sc in each of next 24sc.

Rnd 38: *1sc in each of next 5sc, skip next sc, rep from * around (20 sc).

Rnd 39: 1sc in each of next 20sc.

Rnd 40: *1sc in each of next 4sc, skip next sc, rep from * around (16 sc).

Rnd 41: *1sc in each of next 3sc, skip next sc, rep from * around (12 sc).
Stuff the body.

Rnd 42: *1sc in each of next 2sc, skip next sc, rep from * around (8 sc).

Rnd 43: *1sc in next sc, skip next sc, rep from * around until the ring is closed.

Fasten off and weave in the end.

EARS
Make 2 alike.
Foundation row: Beg at the base of the ear—where it joins the head, using yarn MC and G-6 (4.00 mm) hook, make 2ch.
Rnd 1: 6sc in 2nd ch from hook.
Rnd 2: [1sc in next sc, 2sc in next sc] 3 times (9 sc).
Rnd 3: 1sc in each of next 9sc, turn. Now work in rows.
Row 1: 1ch, 1sc in each of next 8sc, turn (8 sc).
Row 2: Sl st in first sc, 1ch, 1sc in each sc across, turn (7 sc).
Rep last row 6 times more.
Rim of ear
Next rnd: Work in sc evenly from the point around edge of ear and back to the point, sl st in first sc.
Fasten off.

HORNS
Make 2 alike.
Foundation row: Beg at the top of the horn, using yarn MC and G-6 (4.00 mm) hook, make 2ch.
Rnd 1: 3sc in 2nd chain from hook, sl st in first top of first sc, make 9ch.
Fasten off, leaving a tail end with which to sew on the head.

SMALL SPOTS
Make 2 alike.
Foundation row: Using yarn A and G-6 (4.00 mm) hook, make 4ch, join with sl st in first ch to form ring.
Rnd 1: Working over loose end, 1ch, 8sc into ring (8 sc).
Rnd 2: [1sc in next sc, 2sc in next sc] 4 times, sl st in top of first sc (12 sc).**
Fasten off. Pull up the center tail end to close the ring, sew onto the neck with the other tail end.

BIG SPOTS
Make 2 alike.
Work as for "Small Spots" up to ** (12 sc).
Rnd 3: [1sc in each of next 2sc, 2sc in next sc] 4 times, sl st in top of first sc (16 sc).
Fasten off. Pull up the center tail end to close the ring, sew onto the neck and body with the other tail end.

HOOVES
Make 4 alike.
Foundation row: Using yarn B and G-6 (4.00 mm) hook, make 2ch.
Rnd 1: 8sc in 2nd ch from hook.
Rnd 2: 2sc in each of next 8sc (16 sc).
Rnd 3: 1sc in each of next 16sc.
Rep last rnd 5 times more.
Rnd 9: [1sc in next sc, skip next sc] 8

times, sl st in top of first sc (8 sc).
Fasten off.

HIND LEGS
Make 2 alike.
Foundation row: Using yarn A and G-6 (4.00 mm) hook, make 28ch.
****Row 1:** 1sc in 2nd ch from hook, 1sc in each ch across, turn.
Rnd 2: 1ch, 1sc in each sc across, turn.
Rep last row twice more.
Fasten off. **

FORELEGS
Make 2 alike.
Foundation row: Using yarn MC and H-8 (5.00 mm) hook, make 28ch.
Make as for hind leg from ** to **.

TAIL
Foundation row: Using yarn MC and G-6 (4.00 mm) hook, make 10ch. Fasten off.
Cut short lengths of yarn B and sew to one end of tail to create a fringe.

TO FINISH
Using yarn MC, stitch a French knot at either side of the head, then sew a bead under each knot to make the eyes.
Using black sewing thread used double, sew a fan of short stitches above the French knot as eyelashes. Using brown embroidery thread or yarn, sew 2

straight stitches to nose for nostrils. Using pink embroidery thread or yarn, sew a stem stitch mouth under nose. Sew the ear base to the back/side of the head, sew the horns to the top of the head. Sew the chin to the neck to pull head down slightly.

Sew up the back seam of each leg. Stuff each hoof, insert the legs just into open end of the hoof and sew in place—the legs may need pressing to stop them from curling, but read the manufacturer's guidelines before doing so.

Sew on tail. Tie ribbon in a bow to one horn.

Gown & Scarf

MATERIALS

- **RYC** *Cashcotton 4ply*
  One ball of Cyclamen 00911 (MC)
- **Rowan** *Lurex Shimmer*
  One ball of Pewter 333 (A)
- **GGH** *Handknit Amelie*
  One ball of Magenta 004 for scarf (B)
- Hook size: H-8 (5.00 mm)
- Yarn needle

GAUGE

13 sts and 12 rows measured over 2 in (5 cm) working single crochet in MC and using H-8 (5.00 mm) hook.

GOWN

(Back and front worked in one piece.)

Foundation row: Beg at the hem edge, using yarn MC, make 49ch.

Row 1: 1sc in 2nd ch from hook, 1sc in each ch across, turn (48 sc).

Row 2: 1ch, 1sc in each sc across, turn. Rep last row 3 times more.

Fasten off yarn MC, join in yarn A and rep last row 5 times more.

Fasten off yarn A, join in yarn MC and rep last row 5 times more.

Fasten off yarn MC, join in yarn A and rep last row 5 times more.

Fasten off yarn A, join in yarn MC and cont as follows:

Row 21: 1ch, *1sc in each of next 3sc, skip next sc, rep from * across, turn (36 sc).

Row 22: 1ch, 1sc in each sc across, turn (36 sc).

Rep last row twice more.

Row 25: 1ch, *1sc in each of next 2sc, skip next sc, rep from * across, turn (24 sc).

Row 26: 1ch, [1sc in each of next 4sc, skip next 6sc, make 6ch] twice, 1sc in each of next 4sc.

Fasten off.

TO FINISH

Using MC yarn, sew up the back seam, weave in ends.

SCARF

Foundation row: Using yarn B, make 35ch.

Row 1: 1sc in 2nd ch from hook, 1 sc in each ch across (34 sc).

Row 2: 1ch, 1sc in each sc across. Fasten off. Weave in ends.

Mama Duck & Pom-Pom Chick

Whether propped on a bookshelf or a bedside table, this maternal duck is a delightful addition to any child's room. The young hatchling is so easy to create out of pom-poms, you may want to make him a couple more friends in your favorite colors!

FINISHED SIZES
Mama Duck: 12 × 6 in (30 cm × 15 cm)
Pom-Pom Chick: 2½ in (6 cm) diameter

MATERIALS
- **RYC** *Luxury Cotton DK*
  One ball of Tang 252 for Mama Duck (MC)
- **Adriafil** *Angora Carezza*
  Small amount of Brown 87 for bill & legs (A)
  One ball of Orange 85 for feet and chick (B)
- Hook: G-6 (4.00 mm) and E-4 (3.50 mm)
- 1¾ in (4.5 cm) diameter pom-pom maker, or two circular pieces of cardboard cut to 1¾ in (4.5 cm) diameter with ¾ in (2 cm) diameter hole cut out in the center
- 1¼ in (3 cm) diameter pom-pom maker, or two circular pieces of cardboard cut to 1¼ in (3 cm) diameter with ⅜ in (10 mm) diameter hole cut out in the center
- Polyester toy fiberfill or batting
- Yarn needle

GAUGE
9 sts and 10 rnds measured over 2 in (5 cm) working single crochet and using G-6 (4.00 mm) hook.

NOTE:
Before beg the second rnd in each section, place a marker or short length of contrasting yarn across your crochet and up against the loop on the hook and above the working yarn. Work Rnd 2 then slip the marker out and place it at the beg of the next rnd and so on. The marker will indicate where each subsequent rnd starts.

Mama Duck

HEAD & BODY
Using yarn MC and G-6 (4.00 mm) hook, beg at the top of the head, make 3ch.
Foundation rnd: Working over tail end, 8sc in 3rd ch from hook, join to top of 3ch with sl st to form ring (8 sc).
Shape beneath head
Rnd 1: 2sc in each of next 4sc, 1sc in each rem sc around (12 sc).
Rep last round once more (16 sc).

Rnd 3: 1sc in each of next 16sc.
Rep last rnd 3 times more.
Shape neck
Rnd 7: *1sc in each of next 3sc, skip next sc, rep from * around (12 sc).
Rnd 8: 1sc in each of next 12sc.
Rep last rnd twice more.
Shape body
Rnd 11: 1sc in each of next 4sc, 2sc in each of next 6sc, 1sc in each of next 2sc (18 sc).
Rnd 12: 1sc in each of next 18sc.
Rep last rnd twice more.
Rnd 15: [1sc in next sc, skip next sc] twice, [1sc in next sc, 2sc in next sc] 4 times, [1sc in next sc, skip next sc] twice, 1sc in each of next 2sc (19 sc).
Rnd 16: 1sc in each of next 19sc.
Rep last rnd twice more.
Rnd 19: 2sc in each of next 5sc, [1sc in each of next 2sc, 2sc in next sc] twice, [1sc in next sc, 2sc in next sc] 4 times (30 sc).
Rnd 20: 1sc in each of next 30sc.
Rnd 21: *1sc in each of next 2sc, 2sc in next sc, rep from * around (40 sc).
Rnd 22: 1sc in each of next 40sc.
Rnd 23: [1sc in next sc, skip next sc] 4

times, 2sc in next sc, [1sc in each of next 2sc, 2sc in next sc] 8 times, [skip next sc, 1sc in next sc] 3 times, skip last sc (41 sc).

Rnd 24: 1sc in each of next 41sc.

Rep last round 3 times more.

NOTE: *The next 6 rnds create the "fan" tail.*

Rnd 28: [1sc in next sc, skip next sc] 4 times, [1sc in each of next 2sc, 2sc into next sc] 8 times, 1sc in each of next 2sc, [skip next sc, 1sc in next sc] 3 times, skip last sc (41 sc).

Rnd 29: 1sc in each of next 41sc.

Rep last two rnds twice more.

Rnd 34: 1sc in each of next 41sc.

Rep last rnd once more.

Fasten off.

WINGS

Make 2 alike.

Using yarn A and G-6 (4.00 mm) hook, beg at the top of the wing and starting with a long tail end, which will be used to tie up the wings at the back, make 15ch.

Row 1: 1sc in 2nd ch from hook, 1 sc in each ch across, turn (14 sc).

Row 2: 1ch, skip first sc, 1sc in each sc to last sc, skip last sc, turn (12 sc).

Rep last row 4 times more (4 sc).

Fasten off.

BILL

Using yarn A and E-4 (3.50 mm) hook, make 3ch.

Foundation rnd: Working over tail end, 8sc in 3rd ch from hook, join to top of 3ch with sl st to form ring (8 sc).

Rnd 1: 1sc in each sc around.

Rep last rnd 4 times more.

Fasten off.

LEGS

Make 2 alike.

Using yarn A and G-6 (4.00 mm) hook, make 23ch.

Row 1: 1sc in 2nd ch from hook, 1 sc in each ch to last ch, sl st in last ch.

Fasten off.

FEET

Make 2 alike.

Using yarn B and G-6 (4.00 mm) hook, make 12ch.

Row 1: 1 sc in 2nd ch from hook, 1 sc in each of next 4ch, make 6ch, 1 sc in 2nd ch from hook, 1 sc in each of next 4 ch, 1 sc in each of next 5 ch, sl st in last ch.

Fasten off.

TO FINISH

Using a blunt-ended yarn needle and MC yarn, sew the tail end together, leaving a gap. Then stuff the head, neck, body, and tail, manipulating the fiberfill to give the duck its shape. Sew the gap closed.

Stuff the bill lightly, then oversew the bill to the front of the head. Using yarn A, stitch a French knot eye to each side of the head.

Sew on each wing with one of the row ends joined to one side of the straight part of the back. The loose tail end can be tied to join the two points of each wing to hold in the chick.

Attach one of the ends of each leg to the underbelly, about 1½ in (4 cm) apart. Attach the other end to the middle of the "T" shape of the foot.

Pom-Pom Chick

Using the larger of the pom-pom templates and yarn B, wind the yarn around the two pom-pom templates from one end to the other. If using a cardboard template, place the two pieces together and wind the yarn through the hole in the center until the yarn feels thick on the template. Cut in between the templates, attach a length of strong yarn between the open cut ends of the yarn, and tie firmly. Open and remove the templates. Trim the pom-pom as close as you can to the center, creating a tail shape on one side.

Make the smaller pom-pom in the same manner, trimming the head as short as you can. Using yarn A, sew on a closed eye at each side of the head. To make the bill, using yarn A and E-4 (3.50 mm) hook, make 4 ch, weave in the loose end, bend the bill in half, and sew the middle fold onto the front of the pom-pom.

Larry the Lobster

Bold and cheerful, this boisterous double-crocheted lobster looks as comfortable on rocky, muddy shorelines as he does in your child's warm embrace. This snazzy scavenger may have giant claws and wiry legs, but he's deceptively cuddly!

FINISHED SIZE
16 in (41 cm) long × 15 in (38 cm) wide (claws outstretched)

MATERIALS
- **Lobster Pot** *Bulky*
  One ball of Lobster Bisque
- Two ¼ in (6 mm) black glass beads or similar for eyes
- Hook: N-15 (10.00 mm)
- Polyester toy fiberfill or batting
- Yarn needle

GAUGE
9 sts and 8 rnds measured over 2 in (5 cm) working single crochet in MC and using N-15 (10.00 mm) hook.

NOTE:
Before beg the second rnd in each section, place a marker or short length of contrasting yarn across your crochet and up against the loop on the hook and above the working yarn. Work Rnd 2 then slip the marker out and place it at the beg of the next rnd and so on. The marker will indicate where each subsequent rnd starts.

BODY
Foundation row: Beg at the tail, make 9ch.
Row 1: 1sc in 3rd ch from hook, 1 sc in each of next 5ch, skip last ch, turn (6 sc).
Row 2—4: 1ch, 1sc in each sc across, turn.
Row 5: Make 6ch, skip first 5sc, sl st in last sc (12 sts).
Cont to work in rnds.
Rnd 1: 1sc in top of each of next 6sc, 1sc in each of next 6ch (12 sc).
Rnd 2: 1sc in each sc around.
Rep last rnd once more.
Rnd 4: 1sc in top of each sc around.
Rep last 3 rnds twice more.
Shape thorax
Rnd 11: *1sc in each of next 2sc, 2sc in next sc, rep from * around (16 sc).
Rnd 12: 1sc in each sc around.
Rep last rnd twice more.
Rnd 15: *1sc in each of next 3sc, skip next sc, rep from * around (12 sc).
Rnd 16: 1sc in each next sc around.
Rep last rnd twice more.
Shape head
Rnd 19: *1sc in each next 2sc, skip next sc, rep from * around (8 sc).

Rnd 20: [1sc in each of next 3sc, skip next sc] twice (6 sc).
Carefully turn out to other side, sew the edge of the abdomen at Rnd 1 to join with the top of the tail. Stuff the tail a little, then the body and the head.
Rnd 21: *1sc in next sc, skip next sc, rep from * until gap is closed.
Fasten off.

CLAWS
Make 2 alike.
Foundation row: Beg at the body end, make 2ch.
Rnd 1: 6sc in 2nd ch from hook.
Rnd 2 and 3: 1sc in each of next 6sc.
Rnd 4: *1sc in next sc, 2sc in next sc, rep from * around (9 sc).
Rnd 5: *1sc in each of next 2sc, 2sc in next sc, rep from * around (12 sc).
Rnd 6: *1sc in next sc, skip next sc, rep from * around (6 sc).
Shape large claw
Rnd 7: *1sc in next sc, 2sc in next sc, rep from * around (9 sc).
Rnd 8: 1sc in each of next 4sc, 2sc in next sc, 1sc in each of next 4sc (10 sc).

Rnd 9: 1sc in each of next 4sc, 2sc in each of next 2sc, 1sc in each of next 4sc (12 sc).

Rnd 10: 1sc in each of next 4sc, 2sc in each of next 4sc, 1sc in each of next 4sc (16 sc).

Rnd 11: 1sc in each of next 16sc.

Rnd 12: *1sc in each of next 3sc, skip next sc, rep from * around (12 sc).

Rnd 13: *1sc in each of next 2sc, skip next sc, rep from * around (8 sc).

Rnd 14: 1sc in each of next 8sc.

Shape large claw

Rnd 15: 1sc in each of next 8sc, turn. Cont to work in rows.

Row 1: 1ch, 1sc in each of next 5sc, turn. Rep last row once more.

Row 3: Sl st in first sc, 1ch, 1sc in each of next 2sc, skip next sc, 1sc in last sc, turn (3 sc).

Row 4: Sl st in first sc, 1ch, 1sc in next sc (1 sc).

Fasten off.

SMALL CLAW

Foundation row: Beg at the body end, make 6ch.

Row 1: 1sc in 2nd ch from hook, 1sc in each ch across, turn (5 sc).

Row 2: Sl st in first sc, 1ch, 1sc in each of next 2sc, skip next sc, 1sc in last sc, turn (3 sc).

Row 3: Sl st in first sc, 1ch, skip next sc, 1sc in last sc, turn (1 sc).

Row 4: 1ch, 1sc in next sc.

Fasten off.

LEGS

Make 8 alike.

Foundation row: Beg at the body end, make 10ch.

Fasten off.

Snip one tail end to about ¾ in (2 cm), use the other to sew onto the body.

TO FINISH

For the rings around the tail make three lengths of 16ch. Sew each chain of 16 around the tail along where rnds have been worked into top of sc only.

Cut two 12 in (30 cm) lengths of yarn for the antennae and sew to front of face, then sew the eyes just above these.

Sew up the large pincers along row ends, leaving a small gap for stuffing each claw. Stuff the first part of the claws, leaving pincers unstuffed. Close gaps, shape pincers to a point.

Sew the claws to the body near the eyes, referring to the photograph for positioning. Sew the legs, four on each side of the body, three pairs toward the head and last pair just above where the tail meets the body. Fold each small pincer in half widthways across the foundation row, sew up along row ends, lightly shape into a point with your fingers. Sew a small pincer to the top of each claw.

Sir Waldorf Walrus

Even though he's a softy, such a grand, formidable creature deserves a title of honor! Waldorf will quickly become a firm favorite among little ones. With his long tusks and soft belly, this creature of the deep makes an intriguing and fun playmate.

FINISHED SIZE
13½ in (34 cm) long

MATERIALS
- **RYC** *Cashsoft Aran*
  One ball of Mole 003 (MC)
  One ball of Cream 013 for cheeks (A)
- **Anchor** *Tapisserie Wool*
  One skein of 8036 (B)
- Hook: K-10½ (6.50 mm) and H-8 (5.00 mm)
- Two ³/₁₆ in (5 mm) buttons for eyes
- Brown yarn for nose
- Black sewing thread for whiskers and for attaching buttons
- Polyester toy fiberfill or batting
- Yarn needle

GAUGE
7 stitches and 6½ rows measured over 2 in (5 cm) working in single crochet in yarn MC and using K-10½ (6.50 mm) hook.

NOTE:
Before beg the second rnd in each section, place a marker or short length of contrasting yarn across your crochet and up against the loop on the hook and above the working yarn. Work Rnd 2 then slip the marker out and place it at the beg of the next rnd and so on. The marker will indicate where each subsequent rnd starts.

HEAD & BODY
Foundation row: Beg at the head, using yarn MC and K-10½ (6.50 mm) hook, make 2ch.

Rnd 1: 6sc in 2nd ch from hook.

Rnd 2: 2sc in each of next 6sc (12 sc).

Rnd 3: *1sc in next sc, 2sc in next sc, rep from * around (18 sc).

Rnd 4: *1sc in each of next 2sc, 2sc in next sc, rep from * around (24 sc).

Rnd 5: 1sc in each sc around.
Rep last rnd 5 times more.

Shape body

Rnd 11: 2sc in each of next 12sc, [1sc in next sc, skip next sc] 6 times (30 sc).

Rnd 12: 1sc in each sc around.
Rep last rnd 5 times more.

Rnd 18: 2sc in each of next 18sc, [1sc in next sc, skip next sc] 6 times (42 sc).

Rnd 19: 1sc in each sc around.
Rep last rnd 5 times more.

Rnd 25: *1sc in each of next 2sc, skip next sc, rep from * around (28 sc).

Rnd 26: 1sc in each sc around.

Rnd 27: *1sc in each of next 6sc, skip next sc, rep from * around (24 sc).

Rnd 28: 1sc in each sc around.

Rnd 29: *1sc in each of next 5sc, skip next sc, rep from * around (20 sc).
Stuff the walrus up to this row, then cont as follows:

Rnd 30: 1sc in each sc around.

Rnd 31: *1sc in each of next 4sc, skip next sc, rep from * around (16 sc).

Rnd 32: 1sc in each sc around.

Rnd 33: *1sc in each of next 3sc, skip next sc, rep from * around (12 sc).

Rnd 34: 1sc in each sc around.

Rnd 35: *1sc in each of next 4sc, skip next sc, rep from * around (6 sc).

Rnd 36: 1sc in each sc around.

Rep last rnd 5 times more.

Stuff the last of the body.

Rnd 42: *1sc in next sc, skip next sc, rep from * around until the ring is closed.
Fasten off.

CHEEKS

Make 2 alike.

Foundation row: Beg at the head, using yarn A and H-8 (5.00 mm) hook, make 2ch.

Rnd 1: 6sc in 2nd ch from hook.

Rnd 2: 2sc in each of next 6sc (12 sc).

Rnd 3: 1sc in each sc around.

Rnd 4: *1sc in next sc, 2sc in next sc, rep from * around (18 sc).

Rnd 5: 1sc in each sc around.

Rnd 6: *1sc in next sc, skip next sc, rep from * around (9 sc).

Stuff with a matching yarn to pad out.

Rnd 7: *1sc in next sc, skip next sc, rep from * until the ring is closed. Fasten off.

FRONT FINS

Make 2 alike.

Foundation row: Using yarn A and H-8 (5.00 mm) hook, beg at the part of fin that is later sewn to body, make 8ch.

Row 1: 1sc in 2nd ch from hook, 1sc in each ch across, turn (7 sc).

Row 2: 1ch, 1sc in each sc across, turn.

Row 3: 2ch, 1dc in each sc across, turn.

Row 4: 2ch, 1hdc in each of next 4dc, 1sc in each of next 3dc, turn.

Row 5: 1ch, 1sc in each of next 3sc, 1hdc in each of next 4hdc, turn.

Row 6: 2ch, 1hdc in each of next 4hdc, 1 sc in each of next 3sc.
Fasten off.

TAIL FINS

Make 2 alike.

Foundation row: Using yarn MC and H-8 (5.00 mm) hook, beg at the part of fin that is later sewn to body, make 5ch.

Row 1: 1sc in 2nd ch from hook, 1sc in each ch across, turn (4 sc).

Row 2: 1ch, 1sc in each sc across, turn.

Row 3: 2ch, 1dc in next sc, 1hdc in next sc, 1sc in each of next 2sc.
Fasten off.

TUSKS

Make 2 alike.

Foundation row: Using yarn B and H-8 (5.00 mm) hook, beg at the part of fin that is later sewn to body, make 13ch.

Row 1: 1sc in 2nd ch from hook, 1sc in each ch across.
Fasten off, leaving the tail ends.

TO FINISH

Using matching yarn sew, the front fins onto each side of the body, curving the fin slightly as you stitch—so that you've sewn in an arc shape. Sew the two tail fins at either side at the end of the tail. Sew the cheeks onto the front of the head, then sew these together where they meet. Using brown yarn, over-sew nose, catching the cheeks on each side. Using black thread, sew a few loose running stitches on each cheeks to form whiskers.

Sew on the two button eyes at either side of the head. Sew on the tusks under the cheeks, using the tail ends—you may wish to press these with a cool iron if they curl a little, but check the yarn manufacturer's guidelines first.

Pinch the middle of the back to "pull up" the walrus's back a little then using matching yarn, sew a few discreet stitches to hold in place.

Mickey the Marmoset

Mickey's a cheeky character that will inspire your tot to have lots of fun. Soft, cuddly, and totally friendly with long, wraparound arms and legs and an endearing face—why not make a few more and create a playful troop of your own?

Marmoset

FINISHED SIZE

17 in (43 cm) long × 19¾ in (50 cm) wide (arms outstretched)

MATERIALS

- **Rowan** *Soft Baby*
  One ball of Princess 003 (MC)
- **Anchor** *Tapisserie Wool*
  One skein of Cyclamen Pink 8452 for head and body (A)
  Two skeins of Rose Pink 8454 for nose and tail (B)
- Hook: H-8 (5.00 mm)
- Small pieces of felt for eyes
- Black thread for sewing on eyes, nose, and mouth
- Two ¼ in (6 mm) black glass beads or similar for eyes
- Polyester toy fiberfill or batting
- Yarn needle

GAUGE

12 sts and 9 rnds measured over 2 in (5 cm) working single crochet in MC and using H-8 (5.00 mm) hook.

NOTE:

Before beg the second rnd in each section, place a marker or short length of contrasting yarn across your crochet and up against the loop on the hook and above the working yarn. Work Rnd 2 then slip the marker out and place it at the beg of the next rnd and so on. The marker will indicate where each subsequent rnd starts.

HEAD & BODY

Foundation rnd: Using yarn A, beg at the nose end, make 4ch, join with a sl st to form ring.

Rnd 1: Working over tail end, [1sc in next ch, 2sc in next ch] twice (6 sc).

Rnd 2: 1sc in each of next 6sc.

Rnd 3: 2sc in each of next 6sc (12 sc).

Rnd 4: 1sc in each of next 12sc.

Break off yarn A.

Top of nose shaping

Rnd 5: Join in yarn MC, 2sc in each of next 10sc, 1sc in each of next 2sc (22 sc).

Rnd 6: 1sc in each of next 7sc, 2sc in each of next 5sc, 1sc in each of next 10sc (27 sc).

Break off yarn MC.

Rnd 7: Join in yarn B, 1sc in each of next 27sc.

Rep last round 3 times more.

Rnd 11: *1sc in each of next 2sc, skip next sc, rep from * around (18 sc).

Rep last round once more (12 sc).

Rnd 13: 1sc in each of next 12sc.

Rep last round once more.

Break off yarn B.

Rnd 15: Join in yarn MC, 1sc in each of next 12sc.

Stuff the head.

Body shaping

Rnd 16: *1sc in next sc, 2sc in next sc, rep from * around (18 sc).

Rnd 17: 1sc in each sc around.

Rep last 2 rnds once more (27 sc).

Rnd 20: 1sc in each sc around.

Rep last rnd 9 times more.

Rnd 30: *1sc in each of next 2sc, skip next sc, rep from * around (18 sc).

Rep last rnd once more (12 sc).

Stuff the body.

Rnd 32: Sl st every other sc around until the body opening is closed. Fasten off.

EARS

Make 2 alike.

Foundation rnd: Using yarn MC, make 4ch, join with a sl st to form ring.

Rnd 1: Working over tail end, [1sc in next ch, 2sc in next ch] twice (6 sc).

Next row: 2sc in each of next 6sc, turn (12 sc).

Next row: [1sc in each of next 2sc, skip next sc] 4 times (8 sc).

Fasten off.

ARMS

Make 2 alike.

Using yarn MC make 3ch.

Foundation rnd: Working over tail end, 8sc in 3rd ch from hook (8 sc).

Rnd 1: 1sc in each of next 8sc.

Rnd 2: 2sc in each of next 8sc (16 sc).

Rnd 3: *1sc in next sc, skip next sc, rep from * around (8 sc).

Rnd 4: 1sc in each of next 8sc.

Stuff hands.

Rep last rnd until arm measures 6½ in (16 cm).

Next rnd: *1sc in next sc, 2sc in next sc, rep from * around (12 sc).

Rnd 2: 1sc in each of next 12sc.

Rep last rnd until the entire arm measures 9½ in (24 cm).

Fasten off.

LEGS

Make 2 alike.

Using yarn MC make 4ch.

Foundation rnd: Working over tail end, 12sc in 4th ch from hook (12 sc).

Rnd 1: 1sc in each of next 12sc.

Rnd 2: 2sc in each of next 12sc (24 sc).

Rnd 3: 1sc in each of next 24sc.

Rep last rnd twice more.

Rnd 6: *1sc in next sc, skip next sc, rep from * around (12 sc).

Rnd 7: 1sc in each of next 12sc.

Stuff foot.

Rep last rnd until the entire leg measures 9½ in (24 cm).

Fasten off.

TAIL

Using yarn A, make 3ch.

Foundation rnd: Working over tail end, 12sc in 3rd ch from hook (12 sc).

Rnd 1: 1sc in each of next 12sc.

Rep last rnd until tail measures 8¼ in (21 cm). Break off yarn A.

Join in yarn MC and cont with the spiral until the entire tail measures 9¾ in (25 cm).
Fasten off.

TO FINISH

Using a blunt-ended yarn needle and MC yarn, sew two legs to the underside of the body equidistant to one another, and the two arms at either side of the body, two rows beneath the neck color change. Sew the tail between the legs. Roll the first 4¾ in (12 cm) of tail into a coil and sew in place. Sew the base of each ear in place, referring to the photograph for positioning.

Cut out circles of felt ½ in (1 cm) in diameter for the irises. Sew a bead to the center of each iris. Referring to the photograph for placement, sew on the eyes, taking care to sew through only one layer on the marmoset's face. Using black thread and stem stitch, sew on the mouth along first rnd of crochet. Satin stitch a nose in place above the mouth.

Overalls

MATERIALS

- **GGH** *Big Easy*
  One ball of Red 005 (MC)
- Hook: G-6 (4.00 mm)
- Yarn needle

GAUGE

13 sts and 10 rnds measured over 2 in (5 cm) working single crochet in MC and using G-6 (4.00 mm) hook.

SHORTS

Make 2 alike.

Foundation rnd: Using yarn MC, beg at the leg end, make 21ch, join with a sl st to form ring.

Rnd 1: 1ch (does not count as a st), 1sc in each ch around (21 sc).

Rnd 2: 1sc in each of next 21sc.

Rep last rnd 9 times more.

Now work in rows.

Leg shaping

Row 1: 1ch (counts as first st), skip next sc, 1sc in each of next 18sc, turn (19 sts).

Row 2: 1ch, skip next sc, 1sc in each of next 17sc, turn (18 sts).

Row 3: 1ch, skip next sc, 1sc in each of next 16sc, turn (17 sts).

Row 4: 1ch, skip next sc, 1sc in each of next 15sc, turn (16 sts).

Row 5: 1ch, skip next sc, 1sc in each of next 14sc, turn (15 sts).

Row 6: 1ch (does not count as a st), 1sc in each of next 14sc, 1sc in 1ch at beg of previous row, turn (15 sc).

Row 7: 1ch (does not count as a st), 1sc in each of next 15sc, turn.

Rep last row once more.

Fasten off.

TO FINISH

With RS facing, work 1sc along both edges of center front and center back shaping to join both front and back seam.

BIB

With RS and front of trousers facing, count 4sc along last row of left trouser leg, join in yarn MC to this st, 1ch, 1sc in each of next 4sc to front seam, 1sc in each of next 4sc along top of right trouser leg, turn (8 sc).

Next row: 1ch (does not count as a st), 1sc in each of next 8sc, turn.

Rep last row 4 times more.

NOTE: *Do not fasten off.*

Make 17ch for right strap, or until the strap goes from front (top of the bib) over the shoulders and down the back to join the back of the shorts at the waist—you may need to slip the overalls onto the marmoset to accurately measure this.
Fasten off.

Rejoin yarn to other corner of bib, make ch to match other strap and cross the straps over at the back, sew the straps in place at the waist.

Cocoa Koala

G'day, mate! This playful button-nosed marsupial knows how to hang loose! Donning a pretty blue sheath dress accented with pink bows, she's come a long way from home. Your little one is sure to hang onto her forever!

FINISHED SIZE
7¾ in (20 cm) tall

MATERIALS
- **Rowan *Summer Tweed Aran***
  One ball of Hurricane 520 (MC)
- **Jo Sharp Yarns *Kid Mohair***
  Small amount of Light Gray 609 for ears (A)
- Hook: H-8 (5.00 mm) & G-6 (4.00 mm)
- Dark gray DK yarn for nose
- Hot pink lightweight yarn or embroidery thread for mouth
- Yellow embroidery thread for ear bow
- Two ¼ in (6 mm) black glass beads or similar for eyes
- Polyester toy fiberfill or batting
- Yarn needle

GAUGE
9 sc and 8 rnds measured over 2 in (5 cm) working single crochet in MC and using H-8 (5.00 mm) hook.

NOTE:
Before beg the second rnd in each section, place a marker or short length

of contrasting yarn across your crochet and up against the loop on the hook and above the working yarn. Work Rnd 2 then slip the marker out and place it at the beg of the next rnd and so on. The marker will indicate where each subsequent rnd starts.

HEAD
Foundation row: Beg at the nose, using yarn MC and H-8 (5.00 mm) hook, make 2ch.
Rnd 1: 6sc in 2nd ch from hook.
Rnd 2: *1sc in next sc, 2sc in next sc, rep from * around (9 sc).
Rnd 3: 1sc in each sc around.
Rep last rnd twice more.
Shape head
Rnd 6: *1sc in each of next 2sc, 2sc in next sc, rep from * around (12 sc).
Rnd 7: 1sc in each sc around.
Rnd 8: *1sc in each of next 3sc, 2sc in next sc, rep from * around (15 sc).
Rnd 9: 1sc in each sc around.
Using dark gray DK yarn, sew on the nose working a few satin stitches across 3sc of first 3 rnds. Sew on the eyes on each side above the nose. Using pink yarn or embroidery thread, sew a straight stitch for mouth beneath the nose. Stuff the head.
Shape back of head
Rnd 10: *1sc in each of next 2sc, skip

next sc, rep from * around (10 sc).
Rnd 11: *1sc in next sc, skip next sc, rep from * around until ring is closed.
Fasten off. Weave long tail end through to the inside of the head to come out under the chin.

EARS
Make 2 alike.
Foundation row: Using yarn A and G-6 (4.00 mm) hook, make 2ch.
Rnd 1: 6sc in 2nd ch from hook.
Rnd 2: *1sc in next sc, 2sc in next sc, rep from * around (9 sc).
Rnd 3: 1sc in each sc around.
Fasten off. Sew this end to the side of the head.

BODY
Make 2 alike.
Foundation row: Using yarn MC and H-8 (5.00 mm) hook, make 2ch.
Rnd 1: 6sc in 2nd ch from hook.
Rnd 2: 2sc in each of next 6sc (12 sc).
Rnd 3: 1sc in each sc around.
Rep last two rnds once more (24 sc).
Rnd 6: 1sc in each sc around.
Rep last rnd twice more.
Fasten off, leaving long tail end for sewing up front body to back.

ARMS
Make 2 alike.

Foundation row (RS): Beg at the top of the arm, using yarn MC and H-8 (5.00 mm) hook, make 16ch.
Row 1 (WS): 1sc in 2nd ch from hook, 1sc in each ch to end, turn (15 sc).
Row 2 (RS): 1ch, 1sc in each sc to end, turn.
Rep last row 3 times more.
Shape hand
Row 6 (RS): 1ch, 1sc in each of next 3sc, sl st in next sc.
Fasten off, leaving a tail end long enough for sewing the arm seam.
Join other half of hand
With RS facing and working along foundation row edge, count in 4ch from hand end, pull though yarn MC to 4th ch, 1ch, 1sc in each of next 3ch (3 sc).
Fasten off.

LEGS
Make 2 alike.
Foundation row: Beg at toe, using yarn MC and H-8 (5.00 mm) hook, make 2ch.
Rnd 1: 6sc in 2nd ch from hook.
Rnd 2: *1sc in next sc, 2sc in next sc, rep from * around (9 sc).
Rnd 3: 1sc in each sc around.
Rep last rnd 4 times more.
Shape heel
Row 8: 1sc in each of next 4sc, turn.
Row 9: 1ch, 1sc in each of next 4sc, turn.
Rep last row once more.

Fasten off.

Join heel seam—fold the finishing row (last 4sc) in half so that the two ends meet and sew together to form back of heel.

Shape top of foot

Row 11: Join in yarn MC with a sl st at top of heel seam, 1 ch, 1 sc in heel seam, 3sc along 1st row-end edge of heel, 1 sc in each of 5sc across front of foot, then 3sc along 2nd row-end edge of heel (12 sc).

Row 12: 1ch, 1sc in each of next 12sc, turn.

Rep last row until the leg measures 3½ in (9 cm) from toe.

Fasten off, leaving long tail end for sewing up back seam.

TO FINISH

Sew the two body pieces together, RS facing, leave a gap for turning through. Turn RS out and stuff. Close the gap. Sew the underside of the head to the body.

With WS facing, sew up the arms along the seams, leaving a small gap at the hands. Stuff the hands lightly, close the gap. Join to the body just beneath where the head is attached. Lay one hand over the other and sew together at center. Turn each leg WS out, sew up seam. Turn out right way.

Sew a leg to each side of the body with toes pointing to front.

Using a short length of yellow embroidery thread, tie a bow at top of left ear.

Dress

MATERIALS
- **GGH** *Big Easy*
  One ball of Turquoise 021 for top (MC)
- **RYC** *Cashsoft Aran*
  Small amount of Midnight 008 (A)
- Small amounts of any DK yarn for the bows on dress
- Hook: H-8 (5.00 mm)
- Yarn needle

GAUGE

9 sc and 8 rnds measured over 2 in (5 cm) working sc in MC using H-8 (5.00 mm) hook.

Foundation row: Beg at the neck edge, using yarn A, make 16ch.

Row 1: 1sc in 2nd ch from hook, 1 sc in each ch to end, join into a ring with sl st in 1st sc of rnd, taking care not to twist chain (15 sc).

Rnd 1 (Row 2): 1ch, 1sc in each sc around.

Make armholes

Rnd 2: 1sc in each of next 3sc, skip next 2sc, make 2 ch, 1sc in each of next 5sc, skip next 2sc, make 2 ch, 1sc in each of next 3sc, ending with sl st in top of 1st sc. Fasten off yarn A.

Join in yarn MC to same place as sl st was worked.

Rnd 3: 1sc in each of next 3sc, 2sc in next 2ch sp, 1sc in each of next 5sc, 2sc in next 2ch sp, 1sc in each of next 3sc (15 sc).

Rnd 4: *1sc in each of next 2sc, 2sc in next sc, rep from * to end (20 sc).

Rnd 5: 2sc in each sc around (40 sc).

Rnd 6: 1sc in each sc around.

Rep last row 5 times more, ending sl st in first sc of rnd finishing at the back of the dress.

Fasten off and weave in ends.

Tie five small bows over the dress to embellish.

Farmyard & Nursery Toys

Our farmyard friends are designed to be interactive and love to tell bedtime stories. A few nursery toys will add warmth to your child's bedroom and help send your tot to the land of sweet dreams.

Magical Finger Puppets

Easy to make, these four magical characters get a thumb's up on fun! Create the ones here or design your own characters from your favorite film or book. They really are a handful!

FINISHED SIZE

3 × 2¾ in (8 × 7cm) tall

MATERIALS

Wizard
- **Adriafil *Angora Carezza***
  Small amount of Blue 22 (MC)
- **Jaeger *Baby Merino 4-ply***
  Small amount of Dream 123 (A)
- **Anchor *Tapisserie wool***
  Small amount of 8002 for wizard's beard
- Black sewing thread for eyes
- Small amount of silver metallic yarn

Witch
- **Twilley's *Freedom Cotton DK***
  Small amount of Black 14 (MC)
- **Jaeger *Baby Merino 4-ply***
  Small amount of Dream 123 (A)
- **Opal *Uni 4-ply***
  Small amount of Grass Green for hair
- Black sewing thread for eyes and nose
- Orange sewing thread for mouth

Owl
- **RYC *Cashsoft DK* (light worsted)**
  Small amount of Cream 00500 (MC)

- **Anchor *Tapisserie wool***
  Small amount of Cream 8036 for outer eyes (A)
- Small pieces of yellow felt
- Two white feathers
- Black sewing thread for eyes and nose

Walrus Calf
- **Adriafil *Angora Carezza***
  Small amount of Mole 87 (MC)
- **Rowan *Kid Silk Haze***
  Small amount of Pearl 590 (A)
- Cream yarn for tiny tusks
- Embroidery thread for sewing on eyes, nose, and mouth
- Two ¼ in (6 mm) black glass beads or similar for eyes

All versions
Hook size: G-6 (4.00 mm)

GAUGE

12 sts and 12 rows measured over 2 in (5 cm) working single crochet in MC and using G-6 (4.00 mm) hook.

NOTE:

Before beg the second rnd in each section, place a marker or short length of contrasting yarn across your crochet and up against the loop on the hook and above the working yarn. Work Rnd 2 then slip the marker out and place it at the beg of the next rnd and so on. The marker will indicate where each subsequent rnd starts.

Wizard, Witch, & Owl

HEAD & BODY

Foundation row: Using yarn MC, make 12ch. Taking care not to twist the chain, join into a ring with sl st in 1st ch of rnd.

Rnd 1: 1ch, 1sc in each ch around (12 sc).

Rnd 2: 1sc in each sc around.

Rep last row until the body measures 2 in (5 cm).

Shape neck

Next rnd: *Skip next sc, 1sc in each of next 2sc, rep from * around (8 sc).

Next rnd: 1sc in each sc around.

Rep last rnd once more.

Witch and wizard only

Fasten off yarn MC with sl st in next sc, join in yarn A with sl st in same place, make 1ch.

Witch, wizard, and owl

Next rnd: 1sc in each sc around (8 sc).

Next rnd: *2sc in next sc, 1sc in each of next 3sc, rep from * once more (10 sc).
Next rnd: *2sc in next sc, 1sc in each of next 4sc, rep from * once more (12 sc).
Next rnd: *2sc in next sc, 1sc in each of next 5sc, rep from * once more (14 sc).

Witch and wizard only
Use this to coil around in a flat twist at the end of the head. Sew in place to secure. Proceed to instructions for hat.

Owl only
*Skip next sc, 1sc in each of next 6sc, rep from * once more (12 sc).
Next rnd: *Skip next sc, 1sc in each of next 2sc, rep from * around (8 sc).
Next rnd: *Skip next sc, 1sc in next sc, rep from * around until the ring is closed. Fasten off. Weave in ends.

HAT—WITCH & WIZARD ONLY

Fasten off yarn A with sl st in next sc, join in yarn MC with sl st in same place, 1ch.
Next rnd: 1sc in each sc around.
Next rnd: *Skip next sc, 1sc in next sc, rep from * around (7 sc).
Next rnd: 1sc in each sc around.
Rep last rnd twice more.
Next rnd: *Skip next sc, 1sc in next sc, rep

from * around until the ring is closed. Fasten off. Weave in ends.

Witch's hat brim
Foundation row: Using yarn MC, make 15 ch.
Row 1: 1sc in 2nd ch from hook, 2sc in next ch, *1sc in next ch, 2sc in next ch; rep from * to end.
Fasten off. Sew the brim to the top of the head—where the hat rim color begins.

WIZARD & WITCH'S CLOAKS
Foundation row: Beg at the top of collar, using yarn MC, make 11ch.
Row 1: 1sc in 2nd ch from hook, 1sc in each of next 7ch, skip last ch, turn (8 sc).

Row 2: Sl st in first sc, 1ch, 1sc in each of next 6sc, skip last sc, turn (6 sc).
Row 3: 1ch, 1sc in each sc across, turn.
Rep last row 3 times more.
Row 7: 2ch, 1sc in 2nd ch from hook, 1sc in each sc to last sc, 2sc in last sc, turn (8 sc).
Rep last row twice more (12 sc).
Fasten off.
Work a border along each side edge starting at the hem corner and working up to the collar edge—1sc in each sc along.
Fasten off. Weave in ends. Sew in place around the neck edge of the body, leaving upper collar edge free around the back of the head.
Using 2 short lengths of MC, make a tie

at each side of collar and tie at front of cloak.

Using silver metallic yarn, sew a few stars working 3 straight stitches across each other onto the Wizard's robes, cloak, and hat.

TO FINISH
Witch & wizard

Using double thickness black sewing thread, sew two eyes to front of face. Work a split stitch mouth on Witch's face using a length of orange sewing thread. Work 2 straight stitches for eyebrows above eyes on Wizard's face using cream yarn.

For the Wizard's beard, cut 1½ in (3 cm) lengths of cream yarn, thread half of one length through a stitch on the face at the beard position. Re-insert, then re-emerge the needle into the same crochet stitch—the thread should be secure. Trim if necessary. Work a few more lengths in the same way, depending on how bushy you want the beard to be.

For the Witch's hair, cut 1½ in (3 cm) lengths of hair yarn and attach to the back of the head—under the hat brim—in the same way.

Owl

Using outer eye yarn A, make 6ch, join into a ring with a sl st in 1st ch. Fasten off.

Make another the same and sew both in place onto the front of the head. Using black thread, sew two eyes into the center of these outer eyes—making the eyes bigger than that of the wizard's and witch's. Cut out a ¼ in (6mm) equilateral triangle of felt for the beak. Sew onto the owl's face with two black stitches for nostrils. Poke the ends of the feathers into the owl's neck at the side of the body. Sew in place.

Walrus calf

HEAD & BODY

Foundation row: Beg at the head, using yarns MC and A together, make 2 ch.
Rnd 1: 6sc in 2nd ch from hook.
Rnd 2: [1sc in next sc, 2sc in next sc] 3 times (9 sc).
Rnd 3: 1sc in each sc around.
Rep last rnd 3 times more.
Rnd 7: [1sc in next sc, 2sc in next sc] 4 times, 1 sc in last sc (13 sc).
Rnd 8: 1sc in each sc around.
Rep last rnd 3 times more.
Rnd 12: [1sc in each of next 3sc, 2sc in next sc] 3 times, 1 sc in last sc (16 sc).
Rnd 13: 1sc in each sc around.
Rep last rnd once more.
Rnd 15: *1sc in next sc, skip next sc, rep from * around (8 sc).
Rep last rnd twice more (2 sc).

Fasten off. Weave in loose ends.

CHEEKS

Make 2 alike.
Using yarn MC, make 7ch. Fasten off. Use this to coil around in a flat twist at the end of head. Sew in place to secure.

FLIPPERS

Make 2 alike.
Foundation row: In yarn MC, beg at the part of fin which is later sewn to body, make 5ch.
Row 1: 1sc in 2nd ch from hook, 1 sc in each of next 3 ch, turn (4 sc).
Row 2: 1ch, 1sc in each sc across, turn.
Row 3: 1ch, 1sc in each of next 3sc, turn (3 sc).
Row 4: 1ch, 1sc in each sc across, turn.
Row 5: 1ch, 1sc in each of next 2sc, turn (2 sc).
Row 6: 1ch, skip next sc, 1sc in last sc.
Fasten off.

TO FINISH

Sew on the two beads for eyes behind the cheeks. Cut two short lengths of cream yarn and sew securely in place under the cheeks for tusks.
Sew on the flippers with the pointed end facing away from the head. Weave in ends.

Chunky Building Blocks

It's a block party! Learning your A-B-Cs from your 1-2-3s is made super easy with these pastel blocks. It's a great way to use up a yarn stash and a fun accent to any nursery setting.

FINISHED SIZE

All blocks are different sizes as I used all different types of yarn and hooks. This is a great way to use up any leftover yarn from other projects.

MATERIALS

- **Karabella *Aurora Bulky***
  Small amount of Egg Cream 8 for yellow cube
- **Lobster Pot *Bulky***
  Small amount of Hydrangea for turquoise blue cube
- **Rowan *Soft Baby***
  Small amount of Angel 002 for pale blue cube
- Small amounts of any DK or tapestry yarn for letters and numbers
- Hook: H-8 (5.00 mm), I-9 (5.50 mm), L-12 (8.00 mm) and N-15 (10.00 mm)
- Polyester toy fiberfill or batting
- Yarn needle

GAUGE

Gauge is not important for this project as any DK, Chunky, or Super Chunky yarn can be used with respective hook sizes.

BLOCK

Foundation row: Using any yarn and a suitably sized hook, make 6ch.
Row 1: 1sc in 2nd ch from hook, 1sc in each ch across, turn (5 sc).
Rows 2–4: 1ch, 1sc in each sc across, turn (5 sc).
Rnd 5: 1ch, 1sc in each of next 4sc, 3 sc in next (corner) sc, cont around edge making 3sc along left side, 3sc in corner, 3sc across bottom, 3sc in corner, 3sc along right side, 2sc in top right-hand corner, sl st to first sc of rnd.
Weave in ends. Make 5 more squares.

LETTERS & NUMBERS

Decide on a letter or number. Make enough chain to twist and curve into that shape, stitch the chain down onto one or more of the cube faces to secure the shape. For example:
For number "3," using H-8 (5.00 mm) hook, make 18ch, fasten off, leaving a long tail end to sew onto a cube face.

TO FINISH

Sew squares together along outside edges, WS together, and stuff before closing the cube along last edge.

Plush Car & Van

Make a chunky bright blue bubble car and butter-yellow van, or try crocheting one in racy red, marmalade orange or bubblegum pink. Pick a color to suit your mood—or your child's room!

Car

FINISHED SIZE
7¾ in (20 cm) long × 4¼ in (11 cm) wide

MATERIALS
- **Brown Sheep Company** *Lambs Pride Worsted*
  One ball of Brite Blue M-57 for car (MC)
  Small amount of Crème M-10 for roof (A)
- **Cottage Knits** *Chenille*
  One ball of Black for tires (B)
- **Karabella Yarns** *Vintage Cotton*
  Small amount of Calendula 320 for headlights (C)
- Dark gray yarn for window and door detail
- Light gray yarn for door handle detail
- Hooks: H-8 (5.00) and G-6 (4.00 mm)
- Polyester toy fiberfill or batting
- Yarn needle

GAUGE
9 sts and 10 rnds measured over 2 in (5 cm) working single crochet in MC and using H-8 (5.00 mm) hook.

NOTE:
Before beg the second rnd in each section, place a marker or short length of contrasting yarn across your crochet and up against the loop on the hook and above the working yarn. Work Rnd 2 then slip the marker out and place it at the beg of the next rnd and so on. The marker will indicate where each subsequent rnd starts.

SIDES
Make 2 alike.
Foundation row: Beg at the back of the car, using yarn MC and H-8 (5.00 mm) hook, make 8ch.
Row 1: 1 sc in 2nd ch from hook, 1sc in each ch across, turn (7 sc).
Row 2: 1ch, 1sc in each sc to last sc, 2sc in last sc, turn (8 sc).
Row 3: 2ch, 1sc in 2nd ch from hook, 1sc in each sc across (9 sc).
Rep last 2 rows once more (11 sc).
Row 6: 1ch, 1sc in each of next 11 sc across, turn.
Row 7: 2ch, 1sc in 2nd ch from hook, 1sc in each sc across (12 sc).
Row 8: 1ch, 1sc in each of next 12 sc across, turn.
Rep last row 8 times more.

Row 17: Sl st in first sc, 1ch, 1sc in each sc to end, turn (11 sc).
Row 18: 1ch, 1sc in each sc to last sc, skip last sc, turn (10 sc).
Rep last 2 rows twice more (6 sc).
Row 23: 1ch, 1sc in each of next 6 sc, turn.
Row 24: 1ch, 1sc in each sc to last sc, skip last sc, turn (5 sc).
Row 25: 1ch, 1sc in each of next 5 sc, turn.
Rep last row twice more.
Fasten off.

BASE
Foundation row: With yarn MC and H-8 (5.00 mm) hook, make 9ch.
Row 1: 1sc in 2nd ch from hook, 1sc in each ch across, turn (8 sc).
Row 2: 1ch, 1sc in each sc across, turn.
Rep last row 17 times more, or until the length of the base matches the length of one of the sides.

ROOF
Foundation row: With yarn MC and H-8 (5.00 mm) hook, make 9ch.
Row 1: 1sc in 2nd ch from hook, 1sc in each ch across, turn (8 sc).

Row 2: 1ch, 1sc in each sc across, turn.
Rep last row 7 times more, fasten off
yarn MC with sl st.
Join in yarn A with sl st in sl st of
previous row.
Row 10: 1ch, 1sc in each sc across, turn.
Rep last row 9 times more, fasten off
yarn A with sl st.
Join in yarn MC with sl st in sl st of
previous row.
Rep last row 7 times more, or until the
length of the roof fits up the back, over
the top, and down to the front along
one of the car sides.

TIRES

Make 5 alike.
Foundation row: Using yarn B and H-8
(5.00 mm) hook, make 4ch.
Rnd 1: 8sc in 4th ch from hook, working
over loose end—pull up tight when the
tire is complete to close the ring.
Rnd 2: 2sc in each sc around (16 sc).
Rnd 3: 1sc in each sc around.
Rep last rnd twice more.
Rnd 6: [1sc in each of next 2sc, skip next
sc] 5 times, 1sc in last sc (11 sc).
Rnd 7: [1sc in next sc, skip next sc] 5
times, 1sc in last sc (6 sc).

Carefully turn out to RS.

Rnd 8: *Skip next sc, 1sc in next sc, rep from * to end.

Fasten off.

HEADLIGHTS

Make 2 alike.

Foundation row: Using yarn C and H-8 (5.00 mm) hook, make 2ch.

Rnd 1: 6sc in 2nd ch from hook.

Rnd 2: 2sc in each sc around (12 sc).

Rnd 3: 1sc in each sc around (12 sc).

Rep last rnd once more.

Rnd 5: *Skip next sc, 1sc in next sc, rep from * to end (6 sc).

Carefully turn out to RS.

Rep last rnd once more.

Fasten off.

TO FINISH

With RS facing, join each side to the car "roof."

Sew the two headlights onto front of car. Using yarn A, sew 2 straight stitches to each headlight for highlight.

With RS facing sew the base to the rem outer edges of the front, back and sides, leaving a small gap for turning through. Turn RS out, stuff, and close the gap.

Sew on the wheels—two each side and one on the trunk, making sure the wheels on opposite sides are equidistant. Thread a yarn needle with a length of dark gray yarn. Work backstitch down

sides for door and windows and across front for windshield details, as seen in the photograph. Using light gray yarn, sew a straight stitch to each "door" for handle detail.

Van

FINISHED SIZE

9½ in (24 cm) long × 4¾ in (12 cm) wide

MATERIALS

- **Sirdar *Super Chunky***
  One ball of Egg Yolk Yellow 906 (MC)
- **Karabella *Aurora Bulky***
  One ball of White 3 (A)
  One ball of Medium Gray for tires (B)
- **Debbie Bliss *Cashmerino Chunky***
  Small amount of Gray 11-11 for headlights and bumpers (C)
  Gray yarn for window and door detail
- Hooks: K-10½ (6.50 mm) and G-6 (4.00 mm)
- Polyester toy fiberfill or batting
- Yarn needle

GAUGE

7 sts and 6 rows measured over 2 in (5 cm) working single crochet in MC and using K-10½ (6.50 mm) hook.

BACK

Foundation row: Using yarn MC and K-10½ (6.50 mm) hook, make 11ch.

Row 1: 1sc in 2nd ch from hook, 1sc in each ch across, turn (10 sc).

Row 2: 1ch, 1sc in each sc to end, turn.

Rep last row 5 times more.

Change to yarn A, work 4 more rows as last row.

Fasten off.

LEFT SIDE, TOP, & RIGHT SIDE

Foundation row: Beg at left back, using yarn MC and K-10½ (6.50 mm) hook, make 19ch.

Row 1: Sl st in first ch, 1ch, 1sc in each ch across, turn (18 sc).

Row 2: 1ch, 1sc in each sc across, turn.

Row 3: Sl st in first sc, 1ch, 1sc in each sc across, turn (17 sc).

Row 4: 1ch, 1sc in each sc across, turn.

Rep last row 3 times more.

Row 8: Change to yarn A, sl st in first sc, 1ch, 1sc in each sc across (16 sc).

Work 15 more rows as Row 4.

Row 24: Change to yarn MC, 1ch, 1sc in each sc to last sc, 2sc in last sc (17 sc).

Work 2 more rows as Row 4.

Row 27: 2ch, 1sc in 2nd ch from hook, 1sc in each sc across, turn (18 sc).

Row 28: 1ch, 1sc in each sc across, turn.

Rep last 2 rows once more (19 sc).

Fasten off.

FRONT

Foundation row: Using yarn MC and

K-10½ (6.50 mm) hook, make 13ch.

Row 1: 1sc in 2nd ch from hook, 1sc in each ch across (12 sc).

Row 2: 1ch, 1sc in each sc to end, turn. Rep last row 7 times more.

Row 10: Sl st in first sc, 1ch, 1sc in each of next 9sc, skip next sc, 1sc in last sc (10 sc).

Row 11: Change to yarn A, 1ch, 1sc in each sc across.

Fasten off.

BASE

Foundation row: Using yarn MC and K-10½ (6.50 mm) hook, make 11ch.

Row 1: 1sc in 2nd ch from hook, 1sc in each next ch across, turn (10 sc).

Row 2: 1ch, 1sc in each sc across, turn. Rep last row 15 times more.

Fasten off.

Shape front dart

Foundation row: Using yarn A and K-10½ (6.50 mm) hook, make 12ch.

Row 1: 1sc in 2nd ch from hook, 1sc in each ch across, turn (11 sc).

Row 2: 1ch, 1sc in each sc across, turn. Rep last row twice more.

Row 5: Sl st in first sc, 1ch, 1sc in each of next 8sc, skip next sc, 1sc in last sc, turn (9 sc).

Row 6: Sl st in first sc, 1ch, 1sc in each of next 6sc, skip next sc, 1sc in last sc, turn (7 sc).

Row 7: Sl st in first sc, 1ch, 1sc in each of next 4sc, skip next sc, 1sc in last sc, turn (5 sc).

Row 8: Sl st in first sc, 1ch, 1sc in each of next 2sc, skip next sc, 1sc in last sc, turn (3 sc).

Row 9: Sl st in first sc, skip next sc, 1sc in last sc (1 sc).

Fasten off.

Join yarn MC to 1ch at corner of "V"-shaped dart, work 1sc in row ends down two long sides to point of "V." Fasten off, leaving a long tail end for sewing the dart to the front of the van.

WHEELS

Make 5 alike.

Foundation row: Using yarn B and K-10½ (6.50 mm) hook, make 4ch.

Rnd 1: 10sc in 4th ch from hook.

Rnd 2: 2sc in each sc around (20 sc).

Rnd 3: 1sc in each sc around. Rep last rnd once more.

Rnd 5: [Skip next sc, 1sc in each of next 2sc] 6 times, skip next sc, 1sc in last sc (13 sc).

Rnd 6: [Skip next sc, 1sc in next sc] 6 times, skip last sc (6 sc).

Fasten off.

HEADLIGHTS

Make 2 alike.

Foundation row: Using yarn C and G-6 (4.00 mm) hook, make 4ch.

Rnd 1: 8dc in 4th ch from hook, sl st in top of first dc to form ring. Fasten off, leaving long tail end for sewing on.

BUMPERS

Make 2 alike.

Foundation row: Using yarn C and G-6 (4.00 mm) hook, make 21ch.

Row 1: 1sc in 2nd ch from hook, 1sc in each ch across, turn (20 sc).

Row 2: 1ch, 1sc in each sc across, turn. Rep last row 3 times more.

Fasten off. Roll up across the length as you would a sleeping bag, sew along one long end to secure.

TO FINISH

Using a blunt-ended yarn needle and MC yarn, backstitch throughout. Sew the dart to the front of the van. Sew on the two headlights. With RS facing, join the front to the van sides, join the back then the base leaving a small gap at the front for turning through. Stuff the van, then sew up the gap. Sew on the back and front bumpers and then the wheels, adding the fifth tire to the bumper. Thread a yarn needle with a length of gray yarn. Work backstitch down sides for door and windows and across front for windshield details. Using yarn A, embroider a French knot to each headlight for highlights. Using yarn C, embroider a door handle on each side.

Mama Horse & Foal

Mama Horse is a glove puppet, and her young foal is a delightful toy. They can cuddle together when it's time for a tea party or a bedtime story.

FINISHED SIZES
Mama Horse: 13 × 4¾ in (33 × 12 cm)
Foal: 10¼ × 10¼ in (26 × 26 cm)

Mama Horse

MATERIALS
- **Jaeger** *Baby Merino 4ply*
  Two balls of Gold 225 (MC)
- **Artesano** *Alpaca*
  Small amount of Inca Cloud 002 (A)
- **Sirdar** *Snuggly DK*
  One ball of Lilac 219 for mane (B)
- Hook: G-6 (4.00 mm)
- Small pieces of felt in three colors for inner and outer eyes, and nose
- Thread for attaching felt and beads
- Two ¼ in (6 mm) black glass beads or similar for eyes
- Dark brown yarn for mouth
- Two dressmaker's pins
- Yarn needle

GAUGE
9 sts and 10 rows measured over 2 in (5 cm) working single crochet in MC and using G-6 (4.00 mm) hook.

NOTE:
Before beg the second rnd in each section, place a marker or short length of contrasting yarn across your crochet and up against the loop on the hook and above the working yarn. Work Rnd 2 then slip the marker out and place it at the beg of the next rnd and so on. The marker will indicate where each subsequent rnd starts.

HEAD & BODY
Using yarn A, beg at the muzzle end, make 3ch.

Foundation rnd: Working over tail end, 8sc in 3rd ch from hook, join to top of 3ch with sl st to form ring (8 sc).

Rnd 1: 1sc in each of next 8sc.
Rnd 2: 2sc in each of next 8sc (16 sc).
Rnd 3: 1sc in each of next 16sc.
Rnd 4: *1sc in next sc, 2sc in next sc, rep from * around (24 sc).
Rnd 5: 1sc in each of next 24sc, sl st in top of 1st sc.

Shape muzzle
Rnd 6: 1ch, 1sc in same place as sl st was worked, 1sc in each of next 24sc (25 sc).
Rnd 7: Skip the sl st and the 1ch, work 1sc into top of 1st sc of previous rnd, 1sc into each of rem 24sc (25 sc).
Rnd 8: Change to yarn MC, 1dc in each of next 25sc, at the same time catching in the marker.
Rnd 9: 1dc in each of next 24dc, 2dc in last dc (26 dc).
Rnd 10: 1dc in each of next 26dc.
Rnd 11: 1dc in each of next 25dc, 2dc in last dc (27 dc).
Rnd 12: 1dc in each of next 27dc.
Rnd 13: 1dc in each of next 26dc, 2dc in last dc (28 dc).
Rnd 14: 1 dc in each of next 28dc.
Rnd 15: 1dc in each of next 27dc, 2dc in last dc, sl st to top of 1 st dc of rnd (29 dc).

Shape chin
Row 1: 2ch (counts as 1dc), skip dc where sl st was worked, skip next dc, 1dc in each of next 24dc, skip next dc, 1dc in next dc, turn (26 dc).
Row 2: 2ch (counts as 1dc), skip 1st 2dc, 1dc in each of next 23dc, 1dc in top of 2ch at beg of previous row, turn (25 dc).
Row 3: 2ch (counts as 1dc), skip 1st 2dc, 1dc in each of next 22dc, 1dc in top of 2ch at beg of previous row, turn (24 dc).
Row 4: 2ch (counts as 1dc), skip 1st 2dc, 1dc in each of next 21dc, 1dc in top of

2ch at beg of previous row, turn (23 dc).

Row 5: 2ch (counts as 1dc), skip 1st dc, 1dc in each of next 20dc, 2dc in next dc, 1dc in top of 2ch at beg of previous row, join with sl st in top of 2ch at beg of row (24 dc).

Cont to work in spiral rnds (do not turn and keep with RS facing), placing marker at the beg of each rnd for 15 rnds at the same time increasing 2 sts on every 3rd rnd as follows:

Rnd 3: 1dc in each of next 11dc, 2dc in next dc, 1dc in each of next 11dc, 2dc in last dc (26 dc).

Rnd 6: 1dc in each of next 12dc, 2dc in next dc, 1dc in each of next 12dc, 2dc in last dc (28 dc).

Rnd 9: 1dc in each of next 13dc, 2dc in next dc, 1dc in each of next 13dc, 2dc in last dc (30 dc).

Cont increasing as above until there are 34 dc.

Fasten off.

EARS

Make 2 alike.

Using 2 strands—yarn MC and A—together, make 3ch.

Foundation rnd: Working over tail end, 8sc in 3rd ch from hook, join to top of 3ch with sl st to form ring.

Rnd 1: 1sc in each of next 8sc.

Rnd 2: 2sc in each of next 8sc (16 sc).

Rnd 3: 1sc in each of next 15sc, 2sc in next sc (17 sc).

Rnd 4: 1sc in each of next 17sc.

Drop yarn A and cont with yarn MC for the following rows:

Next row: 1sc in each of next 15sc, turn.

Next row: 1ch, skip first sc, 1sc in each of next 11sc, skip next sc, 1sc in next sc, turn (13 sc).

Rep last row 6 times more, working 2sc less before last sc on every row (1 sc).

Fasten off.

TO FINISH

With RS facing, using a blunt-ended yarn needle and matching yarn, backstitch the chin seam.

To mark where to sew on the ears, place the puppet over your hand (seam facing down), carefully pin two dressmaker's pins onto the crochet at the position where your wrist bends—the ears should lie 1 in (2.5 cm) apart with the inner ears facing outwards. Carefully take off the puppet and sew the ears in place with matching yarn around the first row of sc stitches.

Referring to the photograph as a guide, cut out two irises, two pupils, and two nostrils from colored felt.

Join each pupil to its iris by sewing a glass bead to the center.

Referring to the photograph, sew on the felt nostrils and eyes with small stitches around the outer edges, taking care to sew through only one layer on the horse's nose. Using a short length of dark brown yarn, stem stitch a line across the nose to create the mouth.

To attach the mane, cut lengths of yarn B to about 4 in (10 cm). Taking 2 lengths at a time, bend both in half. Use a crochet hook to pull the loop through a dc stitch at the top of the head between the ears. Pass the cut ends through the loops, then pull the cut ends so that the knot lies at the top of the head. Continue with this fringing technique along the top of the head and a little way down the back of the neck.

Foal

MATERIALS

- **Rowan *Soft Baby***
  Two balls of Buttercup 008 (MC)
- **Sidar *Snuggly DK***
  Small amount of Lilac 219 for mane and tail (A)
- **Adriafil *Angora Carezza***
  Small amount of Mink 87 (B)
- Hooks: H-8 (5.00 mm) and G-6 (4.00 mm)
- Small pieces of felt in three colors for inner and outer eyes, and nostrils
- Thread for attaching felt and beads

- Two ¼ in (6 mm) black glass beads or similar for eyes
- Pink yarn for mouth
- Polyester toy fiberfill or batting
- Yarn needle

HEAD & BODY

Using yarn A and H-8 (5.00 mm) hook, beg at the muzzle end, make 3ch.

Foundation rnd: Working over tail end, 8sc in 3rd ch from hook, join to top of 3ch with sl st to form ring (8 sc).

Rnd 1: 1sc in each of next 8sc.

Rnd 2: 2sc in each of next 8sc (16 sc).

Rnd 3: 1sc in each of next 16sc.
Rep last rnd 3 times more ending with sl st in top of 1st sc of rnd.

Rnd 7: Join in yarn MC to same place as sl st was worked, 1sc in each of next 16sc.

Shape nose

Rnd 8: 2sc in each of next 6sc, 1sc in each of next 10sc (22 sc).

Rnd 9: 1sc in each of next 22sc.
Rep last rnd 4 times more.

Rnd 14: [1sc in next sc, skip next sc] 6 times, 1sc in each of next 10sc (16 sc).

Rnd 15: 1sc in each sc around.

Shape chin

Rnd 16: [1sc in each of next 2sc, skip next sc] 5 times, 1sc in next sc (11 sc).

Rnd 17: 1sc in each sc around.
Rep last rnd once more.

Shape neck

Rnd 19: [1sc in each of next 3sc, 2sc in next sc) twice, 1sc in each of next 3sc (13 sc).

Rnd 20: 1sc in each sc around.

Rnd 21: [1sc in each of next 3sc, 2sc in next sc) 3 times, 1sc in next sc (16 sc).

Rnd 22: 1sc in each sc around.

Rnd 23: [1sc in each of next 3sc, 2sc in next sc] 4 times (20 sc).

Rnd 24: 1sc in each sc around.
Rep last rnd 3 times more.

Rnd 28: 1sc in each of next 5sc, [1sc in each of next 2sc, 2sc in next sc] 4 times, 1sc in each of next 3sc (24 sc).

Rnd 29: 1sc in each sc around.
Rep last rnd 3 times more.

Body shaping

Rnd 33: 1sc in each of next 8sc, 2sc in each of next 7sc, 1sc in each of next 9sc (31 sc).

Rnd 34: 1sc in each sc around.

Rnd 35: 1sc in each of next 10sc, 2sc in each of next 11sc, 1sc in each of next 10sc (42 sc).

Rnd 36: 1sc in each sc around.
Rep last rnd 4 times more.

Rnd 41: 1sc in each of next 11sc, [skip next sc, 1sc in next sc] 10 times, 1sc in each of next 11sc (32 sc).

Rnd 42: 1sc in each sc around.

Shape back

Rnd 43: [Skip next sc, 1sc in each of next 3sc] twice, 1sc in each of next 16sc, [skip next sc, 1sc in each of next 3sc] twice (28 sc).

Rnd 44: 1sc in each sc around.

Rnd 45: [Skip next sc, 1sc in each of next 3sc] twice, 1sc in each of next 12sc, [skip next sc, 1sc in each of next 3sc] twice (24 sc).

Rnd 46: 1sc in each sc around.
Rep last rnd 3 times more.

Shape hips

Rnd 50: [1sc in each of next 2sc, 2sc in next sc] 8 times (32 sc).

Rnd 51: [1sc in next sc, 2sc in next sc] 16 times (48 sc).

Rnd 52: 2sc in each of next 10sc, 1sc in each of next 28sc, 2sc in each of next 10sc (68 sc).

Rnd 53: 1sc in each sc around.
Rep last rnd 4 times more.

Rnd 58: *1sc in next sc, skip next sc, rep from * around (34 sc).
Rep last rnd once more (17 sc).
Stuff head and body.

Rnd 60: Sl st every other stitch around until opening is closed.

EARS

Make 2 alike.
Using yarn MC and G-6 (4.00 mm) hook, make 3ch.

Foundation rnd: Working over tail end, 8sc in 3rd ch from hook, join to top of 3ch with sl st to form ring.

Rnd 1: 1sc in each of next 8sc.

Next row: 1sc in each of next 6sc, turn.

Next row: 1ch, 1sc in each of next 6sc, turn.

Next row: 1ch, skip 1st sc, 1sc in each of next 3sc, skip 1sc, 1sc in last sc, turn (4 sc).

Next row: 1ch, skip 1st sc, 1sc in next sc, skip next sc, 1sc in last sc, turn (2 sc).

Next row: Skip 1st sc, sl st in last sc.

Fasten off.

Turn ear inside out.

LEGS

Make 4 alike.

Beg with the hoof, using yarn B and H-8 (5.00 mm) hook, make 3ch.

Foundation rnd: Working over tail end, 8sc in 3rd ch from hook, join to top of 3ch with sl st to form ring.

Rnd 1: 2sc in each of next 8sc (16 sc).

Rnd 2: 1sc in each of next 16sc.

Rep last rnd twice more.

Shape front of hoof

Rnd 5: Skip 1st 2sc, 1sc in each of next 14sc (14 sc).

Rnd 6: Skip 1st 2sc, 1sc in each of next 12sc, sl st to 1st sc (12 sc).

Break off yarn B.

Rnd 7: Join in yarn MC (leg color) to same place as sl st was worked, 1sc in each of next 12sc, sl st to 1st sc.

Rnd 8: 1sc in each of next 12sc.

Shape hoof

Rnd 9: [1sc in next sc, skip next sc] 6 times (6 sc).

Stuff hoof.

Rnd 10: 1sc in each of next 6sc.

Rep last rnd 3 times more.

Shape knees

Rnd 14: [1sc in each of next 2sc, 2sc in next sc] twice (8 sc).

Rnd 15: [1sc in next sc, 2sc in next sc] 4 times (12 sc).

Rnd 16: 1sc in each of next 12sc.

Rnd 17: [1sc in each of next 2sc, skip next sc] 4 times (8 sc).

Rnd 18: [1sc in each of next 3sc, skip next sc] twice (6 sc).

Rnd 19: 1sc in each of next 6sc.

Rep last rnd 5 times more.

Shape top of leg

Rnd 25: [1sc in next sc, 2sc in next sc] 3 times (9 sc).

Rnd 26: 1sc in each of next 9sc.

Rep last rnd 3 times more.

Rnd 30: [1sc in each of next 2sc, skip next sc] 3 times (6 sc).

Stuff lightly.

Sl st every other stitch around until opening is closed.

TO FINISH

Using a blunt-ended yarn needle and MC yarn, sew the four legs to the underside of the body equidistant to one another.

Sew the base of each ear in place referring to the photograph for positioning, taking care not to sew the two sides of the head together.

Referring to the photograph as a guide, cut out two irises, two pupils, and two nostrils from colored felt.

Join each pupil to its iris by sewing a glass bead to the center.

Referring to the photograph, sew on the felt nostrils and eyes with small stitches around the outer edges, taking care to sew through only one layer on the horse's nose. Using a short length of pink yarn, stem stitch a line across the nose to create the mouth.

To attach the mane, cut lengths of yarn to about 4 in (10 cm). Taking two lengths at a time, bend both in half. Use a crochet hook to pull the loop through a sc stitch at the top of the head between the ears. Pass the cut ends through the loops, then pull the cut ends so that the knot lies at the top of the head. Continue with this fringing technique along the top of the head and a little way down the back of the neck.

To attach the tail, follow the instructions for attaching the mane and make the strands twice as long.

Planets & Rocket Mobile

A charged, yarn rocket gently navigates colorful planets to take your little one to the outer limits of dreamland! It's the perfect project for using your yarn stash!

FINISHED SIZES

Planets: about 6½ in (16 cm) diameter
Rocket: about 4¾ in (12 cm) long × 6½ in (16 cm) diameter

MATERIALS

- **Karabella *Aurora Bulky***
  Small amounts of Hot Pink 5, Egg Cream 8, Pistachio 10, Shell Pink 9 for planets
- **Debbie Bliss *Cashmerino Aran***
  Small amount of Red 610 for planet
- **Rowan *Soft Baby***
  One ball of Angel 002
- **Sirdar *Chunky***
  Small amount of Yellow for planet
- **Frog Tree *Chunky***
  Small amount of Navy 37 for planet
- **Cottage Knits *Chenille***
  Small amount of Sky Blue for planet
- **GGH *Samoa-Mouline***
  Small amount of Violet 503 for rocket (MC)
- **Louisa Harding *Kashmir DK***
  Small amount of Lemon 5 for rocket (A)
- **RYC *Silk Wool DK***
  Small amount of Brownstone 308 for rocket base (B)
- Orange DK yarn for flames
- Pale blue DK yarn for hanging threads
- Hooks: K-10½ (6.50 mm), H-8 (5.00 mm) and G-6 (4.00 mm)
- 8 in (20 cm) diameter wooden hoop (or use one half of an embroidery hoop)
- 11 yds (10 m) of ⅜ in (10 mm) wide blue velvet ribbon
- Solvent-free glue stick for stiching the ribbon to the hoop
- Three ⅜ in (10 mm) diameter buttons
- Polyester toy fiberfill or batting
- Yarn needle

GAUGE

Gauge is not necessary here.

NOTE:

Before beg the second rnd in each section, place a marker or short length of contrasting yarn across your crochet and up against the loop on the hook and above the working yarn. Work Rnd 2 then slip the marker out and place it at the beg of the next rnd and so on. The marker will indicate where each subsequent rnd starts.

PLANETS

Make 8 alike—1 in each planet yarn.
Foundation row: Using any chosen planet yarn and K-10½ (6.50 mm) hook, make 4ch.
Rnd 1: 8sc in 4th ch from hook.
Rnd 2: 2sc in each sc around (16 sc).

Rnd 3: 1sc in each sc around.
Rep last rnd twice more.
Rnd 6: [1sc in each next of 2sc, skip next sc] 5 times, 1sc in last sc (11 sc).
Rnd 7: [1sc in next sc, skip next sc] 5 times, 1sc in last sc (6 sc).
Carefully turn out to RS and stuff the planet.
Rnd 8: *Skip next sc, 1sc in next sc, rep from * until ring is closed. Fasten off.

ROCKET

Foundation row: Using yarn MC and H-8 (5.00 mm) hook, make 2ch.
Rnd 1: 4sc in 2nd ch from hook.
Rnd 2: 1sc in each of next 4sc.
Rnd 3: [1sc in next sc, 2sc in next sc] twice (6 sc).
Rnd 4: [1sc in next sc, 2sc in next sc] 3 times (9 sc).
Rnd 5: [1sc in next sc, 2sc in next sc] 4 times, 1 sc in next sc (13 sc).
Rnd 6: [1sc in next sc, 2sc in next sc] 5 times, 1sc in next sc (19 sc).
Rnd 7: 1sc in each sc around.
Rep last rnd twice more. Fasten off yarn MC with sl st in last sc.
Rnd 10: Join in yarn A with sl st in same place as last sl st. Using G-6 (4.00 mm) hook, 1sc in each sc around.
Rep last rnd 5 times more. Fasten off yarn A with sl st in last sc.
Rnd 16: Join in yarn B with sl st in same

place as last sl st. Using H-8 (5.00 mm) hook, 1sc in each sc around.
Rep last rnd 3 times more.
Fasten off.

ROCKET BASE

Foundation row: Using yarn B and H-8 (5.00 mm) hook, make 2ch.
Rnd 1: 4sc in 2nd ch from hook.
Rnd 2: 2sc in each sc around (8 sc).
Rep last rnd twice more (32 sc).
Rnd 5: 1sc in each sc around.
Fasten off.

TO FINISH THE ROCKET

Stuff the rocket. Ease the base of the rocket to just inside the bottom of the rocket base—about ¼ in (6 mm) in. With MC yarn and yarn needle, sew in place. Sew the buttons in a line down the front.
Rocket boosters
Using yarn MC and H-8 (5.00 mm) hook, make 25ch, fasten off. Make another chain in the same manner. Wind one chain around your finger and sew to secure the coil. Do the same to the other chain. Sew each coil to the base of the rocket. Cut lengths of orange yarn and sew to the inside of each booster for flames. Trim.

TO FINISH THE MOBILE

Stick one end of the ribbon to the hoop to secure. Wrap the ribbon around the hoop until it is covered, then cut and secure the end with glue.
Cut the remaining ribbon into five equal lengths for hanging strips.
Glue one end of each of the five ribbon strips to the outside of the hoop at five evenly spaced points around the hoop. Knot the five lengths together at the other end.
Sew differing lengths of pale blue yarn to the top (finishing row) of each planet and to the rocket. Arranging the planets around the hoop as desired, knot each length of yarn securely to the hoop. Tie the rocket to the ribbon so that it hangs down from the center of the mobile.

Pig & Piglet

No playpen would be complete without this heavyweight pair! Both featuring floppy ears and the large one with a couple of brown spots on her back, plump piggies like this could only be stitched in chunky yarn.

FINISHED SIZE
Pig: 16½ × 8¾ in (42 × 22 cm)
Piglet: 6 × 3 in (15 × 8 cm)

MATERIALS
- **Karabella** *Aurora Bulky*
  One ball of Shell Pink 9 (MC)
- **Debbie Bliss** *Cashmerino Aran*
  Small amount of Pink 04-04 (A)
- **GGH** *Velour*
  Small amount of Chocolate 05 (B)
- **Rooster** *Almerino DK*
  One ball of Strawberry Cream 203 (C)
  Small amount of Caviar 206 (D)
- Gray, blue, and cream yarn for eyes
- Dark brown yarn for mouth
- Hook sizes: L-11 (8.00 mm), K-10½ (6.50 mm) and G-6 (4.00 mm)
- Polyester toy fiberfill or batting
- Yarn needle

GAUGE
7 sts and 6 rows measured over 2 in (5 cm) working single crochet in MC and using K-10½ (6.50 mm) hook.

NOTE:
Before beg the second rnd in each section, place a marker or short length of contrasting yarn across your crochet and up against the loop on the hook and above the working yarn. Work Rnd 2 then slip the marker out and place it at the beg of the next rnd and so on. The marker will indicate where each subsequent rnd starts.

Pig

HEAD & BODY

Foundation row: Using yarn MC and L-11 (8.00 mm) hook, beg at the snout, make 2ch.
Rnd 1: 6sc in 2nd ch from hook.
Rnd 2: 2sc in each of next 6sc (12 sc).
Rnd 3: *1sc in next sc, 2sc in next sc, rep from * around (18 sc).
Rnd 4: 1sc in each of next 18sc.
Change to K-10½ (6.50 mm) hook, rep last rnd 4 times more.
Shape top of head
Rnd 9: 2sc in each of next 9sc, 1sc in each of next 9sc (27 sc).
Rnd 10: [1sc in next sc, 2sc in next sc] 9 times, 1sc in each of next 9sc (36 sc).
Rnd 11: 1sc in each of next 36sc.
Shape chin
Rnd 12: 1sc in each of next 27sc, [2sc in next sc, 1sc in next sc] 4 times, 1sc in last sc (40 sc).
Rnd 13: 1sc in each of next 40sc.
Rep last rnd 3 times more.
Shape head
Rnd 17: [1sc in each of next 4sc, skip next sc, 1sc in each of next 3sc, skip next sc] 4 times, 1sc in each of next 3sc, skip next sc (31 sc).
Rnd 18: [1sc in each of next 6sc, skip next sc) 3 times, 1sc in each of next 10sc (28 sc).
Change to L-11 (8.00 mm) hook.
Rnd 19: 1sc in each of next 28sc.
Rep last rnd twice more.
Rnd 22: [1sc in each of next 2sc, skip next sc] 6 times, 1sc in each of next 10sc (22 sc).
Rnd 23: 1sc in each of next 4sc, 2sc in each of next 14sc, 1sc in each of next 4sc (36 sc).
Rnd 24: 1sc in each of next 36sc.
Rep last rnd until the head and body measure 13in (33 cm) from snout to back end.
Stuff the snout, head, and body.
Next rnd: *1sc in each of next 2sc, skip next sc, rep from * around until the gap closes.

Make 15ch for the tail, twist it to curl it a little, fasten off.

LARGE SPOT

Foundation row: Using yarn D and G-6 (4.00 mm) hook, make 2ch.
Rnd 1: 6sc in 2nd ch from hook.
Rnd 2: 2sc in each of next 6sc (12 sc).
Rnd 3: *1sc in next sc, 2sc in next sc, rep from * around (18 sc).**
Rnd 4: *1sc in each of next 2sc, 2sc in next sc, rep from * around (24 sc).
Rnd 5: *1sc in each of next 3sc, 2sc in next sc, rep from * around (30 sc).
Rnd 6: *1sc in each of next 4sc, 2sc in next sc, rep from * around, ending with sl st in top of next sc (36 sc).
Fasten off.

SMALL SPOT

Work as for large spot up to **, ending with sl st in top of next sc.
Fasten off.

EARS

Make 2 alike.
Foundation row: Using yarn A and L-11 (8.00 mm) hook, beg at the top of the ear, make 17ch.
Row 1: 1sc in 2nd ch from hook, 1sc in each of next 12ch, skip next ch, 1sc in last ch, turn (14 sc).
Row 2: 1ch, skip first sc, 1sc in each of next 11sc, skip next sc, 1sc in last sc, turn (12 sc).
Row 3: 1ch, skip first sc, 1sc in each of next 9sc, skip next sc, 1sc in last sc, turn (10 sc).
Row 4: 1ch, skip first sc, 1sc in each of next 7sc, skip next sc, 1sc in last sc, turn (8 sc).
Row 5: 1ch, skip first sc, 1sc in each of next 5sc, skip next sc, 1sc in last sc, turn (6 sc).
Row 6: 1ch, skip first sc, 1sc in each of next 3sc, skip next sc, 1sc in last sc, turn (4 sc).
Fasten off.

HIND LEGS

Make 2 alike.
Foundation row: Using yarn MC and K-10½ (6.50 mm) hook, beg at the base of the trotter, make 2ch.
Rnd 1: 6sc in 2nd ch from hook.
Rnd 2: 2sc in each of next 6sc (12 sc).
Rnd 3: 1sc in each of next 12sc, sl st in top of first sc (12 sc).
Join in yarn B to same place as sl st was worked.
Rnd 4: 1tr in each of next 12sc (12 tr).
Rnd 5: 1tr in each of next 12tr, sl st in top of first tr.
Rnd 6: Join in yarn MC in same place as sl st was worked, 1sc in each of next 12tr (12 sc).

Rnd 7: 1sc in each of next 12sc.
Shape front of leg
Rnd 8: 1sc in each of next 3sc, [1sc in next sc, 2sc in next sc] 3 times, 1sc in each of next 3sc (15 sc).**
Rnd 9: 1sc in each of next 4sc, 2sc in each of next 7sc, 1sc in each of next 4sc (22 sc).
Rnd 10: 1sc in each of next 22sc.
Rep last rnd twice more.
Fasten off.

FORELEGS

Make 2 alike.
Work as for hind leg up to **.
Rnd 9: 1sc in each of next 15sc.
Rep last rnd once more.
Fasten off.

TO FINISH

Sew the ears in place with a decreasing row edge over-sewn onto the top of the head. Around the top edge of the snout, between rows 2 and 4, sew a backstitch line to shape the rim of the snout.

Sew four short rows of gray yarn together to create the eyes. Onto this, sew a French knot in a small length of cream yarn. Make 10ch in a short length of blue yarn and sew around the gray. Sew a mouth across the bottom of the snout using a length of dark brown yarn.

Sew on the spots with WS facing up.

Sew on the hind legs with front facing forward, leaving a gap for stuffing. Stuff the legs then sew up the gap. Sew on the forelegs with front facing you, stuff as before.

Piglet

Make all in one piece.

Foundation row: Using yarn C and G-6 (4.00 mm) hook, beg at the snout, make 4ch.

Row 1: 2sc in 2nd ch from hook, 1sc in next ch, 2sc in last ch, turn (5 sc).

Row 2: 1ch, 2sc in first sc, 1sc in each sc to last sc, 2sc in last sc, turn (7 sc).

Rep last row 4 times more (15 sc).

Row 7: 1ch, 1sc in each of next 15sc, make 7ch for first front leg, turn.

Row 8: 1sc in 2nd ch from hook, 1sc in each of next 5ch, 1sc in each of next 15sc, make 7ch for 2nd front leg, turn.

Row 9: 1sc in 2nd ch from hook, 1sc in each of next 5ch, 1sc in each of next 21sc, turn (27 sc).

Row 10: 1ch, 1sc in each of next 27sc, turn.

Rep last row twice more.

Row 13: 1ch, 1sc in each of next 21sc, turn.

Row 14: 1ch, 1sc in each of next 15sc, turn.

Rep last row 3 times more.

Row 18: 1ch, 1sc in each of next 15sc, make 7ch for first back leg, turn.

Row 19: 1sc in 2nd ch from hook, 1sc in each of next 5ch, 1sc in each of next 15sc, make 7ch for 2nd back leg, turn.

Row 20: 1sc in 2nd ch from hook, 1sc in each of next 5ch, 1sc in each of next 21sc, turn (27 sc).

Row 21: 1ch, 1sc in each of next 27sc, turn.

Rep last row twice more.

Row 24: 1ch, 1sc in each of next 21sc, turn.

Row 25: 1ch, 1sc in each of next 15sc. Fasten off.

EARS

Make 2 alike.

Foundation row: Using yarn C and G-6 (4.00 mm) hook, beg at the base of the ear, make 6ch.

Row 1: 1sc in 2nd ch from hook, 1sc in each of next 4ch, turn (5 sc).

Row 2: 1ch, 1sc in each of next 5sc, turn.

Rep last row twice more.

Row 5: 1ch, skip first sc, 1sc in each of next 2sc, skip next sc, 1sc in last sc, turn (3 sc).

Row 6: 1ch, 1sc in each of next 3sc, turn.

Row 7: 1ch, skip first 2sc, 1sc in last sc. Fasten off.

TO FINISH

With RS facing and using matching yarn and backstitch throughout, fold in half across short row ends, sew around each leg, turn the legs out. Place body and head RS facing, sew along the bottom. Sew along the snout and under the chin, up to first pair of legs. Turn out. Stuff the legs a little, stuff the head and body, sew up the belly.

Using yarn C, make 10ch, join into a ring with a sl st in first ch, fasten off. Sew onto the end of the snout.

Sew the ears in place with base edge sewn onto the top of the head.

Using yarn C, make 10ch, twist the length of crochet, fasten off. Sew one end onto the back of the piglet for the tail.

Using gray yarn, sew the eyes onto the head with straight stitches.

Clover Cow & Calf

Moo-licious! Mummy and her wee one make a lovely pair when out to pasture or in your child's room. Clover boasts a striking allover black-and-white pattern that's accented with pink. Her calf, still wobbly on all fours, makes a fine finger puppet as well!

FINISHED SIZES

Cow: 7½ in (19 cm) long × 4 in (10 cm) wide

Calf: 4½ in (11 cm) long × 2½ in (6.5 cm) wide

MATERIALS

- **Debbie Bliss** *Cashmerino Aran*
  One ball of Black 300300 (A)
  One ball of White 101 (MC)
- **Jaeger** *Pure Cotton DK*
  Small amount of Light Pink 0576 for nose and udder (B)
- Hook: H-8 (5.00 mm)
- Black sewing thread for attaching beads
- Two ¼ in (6 mm) black glass beads or similar for cow's eyes
- Polyester toy fiberfill or batting
- Yarn needle

GAUGE

12 sts and 9 rnds measured over 2 in (5 cm) working single crochet in MC and using H-8 (5.00 mm) hook.

NOTE:

Before beg the first rnd in each section, place a marker or short length of contrasting yarn across your crochet and up against the loop on the hook and above the working yarn. Work Rnd 2 then slip the marker out and place it at the beg of the next rnd and so on. The marker will indicate where each subsequent rnd starts.

Cow

HEAD & BODY

Using yarn B, beg at the nose end, make 3ch.

Foundation rnd: Working over tail end, 8sc in 3rd ch from hook, join to top of 3ch with sl st to form ring (8 sc).

Rnd 1: 1sc in each of next 8sc.

Rnd 2: 2sc in each of next 8sc (16 sc).

Rnd 3: 1sc in each of next 16sc.

Rep last rnd 3 times more ending with sl st in top of last sc of rnd.

Rnd 7: Join in yarn A to same place as sl st was worked, 1sc in each of next 16sc.

Rnd 8: 1sc in each of next 16sc.

Rep last rnd 5 times more, ending with sl st in top of first sc.

Fasten off leaving the marker in the crochet so that you can pick up from there after sewing on face markings.

Add on face markings

Using yarn MC, make 24ch, leaving a long tail end for sewing.

Fasten off.

To sew on the face, thread up one end and secure it at the back of the cow's head.

Curl the chain into a circular shape that resembles the shape in the photograph, catching chain every so often to secure in place.

Referring to the photograph, sew on the nostrils with black yarn, working a couple of straight stitches for each nostril.

Cont with the body

Rejoin yarn A to sl st at end of last rnd on main body.

Shape neck

Rnd 14: *1sc in each of next 3sc, skip next sc, rep from * around (12 sc).

Rnd 15: 1sc in each of next 12sc.

Rnd 16: *1sc in next sc, 2sc in next, rep from * around (18 sc).

Rep last rnd once more (27 sc).

Rnd 18: 1sc in each of next 27sc.
Rep last rnd once more.

Shape belly

Rnd 20: [1sc in each of next 2sc, 2sc in next sc] twice, 1sc in each of next 15sc, [1sc in each of next 2sc, 2sc in next sc] twice (31 sc).

Rnd 21: 1sc in each of next 31sc.
Rep last rnd 16 times more, ending with sl st in top of first sc.
Fasten off, leaving the marker in the crochet so that you can pick up from there after sewing on body markings.

Add on body markings

Using yarn MC, make 50ch, leaving a long loose end for sewing with. Fasten off.
To sew on the body markings, thread up one end and secure it at the back of the cow's body, near the back end.
Curl the chain into a shape that resembles the shape in the photograph, catching chain every so often to secure in place.
Make a second shape with 70ch to sew onto the body near the neck.

Cont with the body

Rejoin yarn A to sl st at end of last rnd on main body.

Shape bottom

Rnd 38: *1sc in each of next 5sc, skip next sc, rep from * to last sc, skip last sc (25 sc).

Rnd 39: *1sc in each of next 4sc, skip next sc, rep from * around (20 sc).

Rnd 40: *1sc in each of next 3sc, skip next sc, rep from * around (15 sc).
Stuff the cow through the bottom.

Rnd 41: *1sc in each of next 2sc, skip next sc, rep from * around (10sc).

Rnd 42: *1sc in next sc, skip next sc, rep from * around until ring is closed.
Fasten off.

TAIL

Using yarn A, make 7ch, join in yarn MC and make 9ch. Fasten off, weaving in the yarn—leave the black tail end for sewing onto the body.
Using yarn MC, make a fringed end at the back (see instructions for fringing technique on page 82).

EARS

Make 2 alike.
Using yarn A, make 16ch.

Row 1: 1sc in 2nd ch from hook, 1sc in each ch across (15 sc).
Fasten off yarn A, join in yarn B.

Row 2: 1sc in each of next 15sc.
Fasten off.

HORNS

Make 2 alike.
Using yarn MC, make 4ch.

Row 1: 1sc in 3rd ch from hook, 1sc in next ch.

Fasten off, leaving the tail ends for sewing onto the head.

BLACK LEGS

Make 3 alike.
Beg with the hoof, using yarn A, make 3ch.

Foundation chain: Working over tail end, 8sc in 3rd ch from hook (8 sc).

Rnd 1: 1sc in each of next 8sc.

Shape sides of hoof

Rep last rnd twice more.

Shape leg

Rnd 4: *1sc in each of next 3sc, skip next sc, rep from * once more (6 sc).

Rnd 5: 1sc in each of next 6sc.**
Rep last rnd until leg measures 4 in (10 cm) from hoof.
Fasten off, leaving the tail ends for sewing onto the body.

BLACK & WHITE LEG

Work as for black leg up to **.

Rnd 6: Join in yarn MC, 1sc in each of next 2sc, change to yarn A to complete the rnd.

Rnd 7: In yarn MC 1sc in each of next 3sc, change to yarn A to complete the rnd.

Rnd 8: In yarn MC 1sc in each of next 4sc, change to yarn A to complete the rnd.

Rnd 9: In yarn MC 1sc in each of next 5sc, change to yarn A to complete the rnd.
Fasten off yarn A.

Rnd 10: In yarn MC 1sc in each of next 6sc.

Rep last rnd until leg measures 4 in (10 cm) from hoof.

Fasten off, leaving the tail ends for sewing onto the body.

UDDER

Foundation row: Using yarn B make 2ch.

Rnd 1: 10sc in 2nd ch from hook (10 sc).

Rnd 2: 2sc in each sc around (20 sc).

Rnd 3: 1sc in each sc around.

Rep last rnd 3 times more.

Fasten off, pull up the loose end at the start to close the ring.

For the teats, cut four lengths of yarn B 4 in (10 cm) long. Secure the ends to the inside of the udder, thread through to the front at the foundation row, and let the threads dangle on the right side. Trim them to ⅜ in (10 cm) from udder.

TO FINISH

Stuff the legs lightly. Using a blunt-ended yarn needle and MC yarn, sew the four legs to the underside of the body equidistant to each other.

Sew each ear together, bending in half widthways, and joining the pink finishing row.

Sew the base of each ear in place, referring to the photograph for accurate positioning.

Sew the widest end of the horns to the top of the head in between the ears.

Sew on a glass bead at either side of the head for the eyes.

Sew the udder to the underside of the cow, about 1 in (2.5 cm) away from the bottom, stuffing it a little before completing the sewing.

Sew the cow's tail to its bottom.

Calf

HEAD & BODY

Foundation chain: Using yarn MC and beg at the tail end, make 9ch, join with sl st in 1st ch to form a ring, taking care not to twist the loop.

Rnd 1: 1sc in each of next 9ch (9 sc).

Rnd 2: *1sc in each of next 2ch, 2sc in next sc, rep from * around (12 sc).

Rnd 3: *1sc in each of next 3sc, 2sc in next sc, rep from * around (15 sc).

Tie yarn A to working yarn, and work it with yarn MC along the back of the work until it is needed.

Rnd 4: In MC 1sc in each of next 4sc, in A 1sc in each of next 2sc, in MC 1sc in each of next 9sc.

Rnd 5: In MC 1sc in each of next 2sc, in A 1sc in each of next 6sc, in MC 1sc in each of next 7sc.

Rnd 6: In MC 1sc in next sc, in A 1sc in each of next 8sc, in MC 1sc in each of next 6sc.

Rnd 7: In MC 1sc in each of next 2sc, in A 1sc in each of next 6sc, in MC 1sc in each of next 7sc.

Rnd 8: In MC 1sc in each of next 4sc, in A 1sc in each of next 2sc, in MC 1sc in each of next 9sc.

Break off yarn A and weave it into the back of the work, cont in yarn MC only.

Rnd 9: 1sc in each of next 15sc.

Rep last rnd 3 times more.

Shape head

Rnd 13: *1sc in each of next 2sc, skip next sc, rep from * around (10 sc).

Rnd 14: 1sc in each sc around.

Rnd 15: *1sc in next sc, skip next sc, rep from * around (5 sc).

Rnd 16: 1sc in each sc around.

Rep last rnd 5 times more.

Rnd 22: *1sc in next sc, skip next sc, rep from * around, rep until ring closes. Fasten off, weave in end.

For the pink disk at the end of the nose, using yarn B, make 2ch, 7sc in 2nd ch from hook ending sl st in top of first sc. Fasten off.

EARS

Make 2 alike.

Foundation chain: Using yarn MC, make 6ch, fasten off.

TAIL

Foundation chain: Using yarn MC, make 10ch, fasten off.

Make a fringed end with 3 lengths of yarn, trimmed to ½ in (12 mm) afterwards (see instructions for fringing technique on page 82).

LEGS

Make 4 alike.

Foundation chain: Using yarn MC, make 9ch.

Row 1: 1sc in 2nd ch from hook, 1sc in each ch across, turn (8sc).

Row 2: 1ch, 1sc in each sc across, turn. Fasten off.

TO FINISH

Sew up the seam at the back of the legs, then, with yarn A sew on a couple of straight stitches at each side of the foot for hooves.

With your finger in the puppet, taking care not to pinch yourself, sew on the two ears joining both ends. Sew on two eyes, stitching a French knot for each with the black yarn. Sew the pink disk to the end of the nose.

Sew on the tail and the legs.

Techniques & Abbreviations

Crochet abbreviations

alt	alt
approx	approximately
beg	beginning
ch	chain(s)
ch sp	chain space(s)
cm	centimeter
cont	continue
dc	double crochet
dc2tog	double crochet two stitches together
dc3tog	double crochet three stitches together
dec	decrease
dtr	double treble
foll	following
hdc	half double crochet
in	inch(es)
inc	increase
m	meters
oz	ounce
patt(s)	pattern(s)
rem	remaining
rep	repeat
RS	right side
sc	single crochet
sc2tog	single crochet two stitches together
sk	skip
sp	space(s)
ss2tog	slip stitch two stitches together
sl st	slip st
st(s)	stitch(es)
tch	turning chain
tog	together
tr	treble
trtr	triple treble
WS	wrong side
yd	yard
yo	yarn over hook (US)
yrh	yarn around hook
[ ]	work instructions in square brackets as directed

Hook conversion

U.S. size	Metric	Old UK/CAN size
–	2.00	14
B/1	2.25	13
–	2.50	12
C/2	2.75	–
–	3.00	11
D/3	3.25	10
E/4	3.50	9
F/5	3.75	–
6	4.00	8
7	4.50	7
H/8	5.00	6
I/9	5.50	5
J/10	6.00	4
K101/2	6.50	3
11	7.00	2
L/12	8.00	0
M/13	9.00	00
N/15	10.00	000
P/16	16.00	–
S	19.00	–

Useful stitches

Backstitch
Use for sewing strong seams or for attaching trims by hand. Bring the needle up from the underside of the fabric and insert it about 1/8 in (3 mm) behind the point at which the thread came out. Bring the needle out about 1/8 in (3 mm) in front of the starting point. Continue in same manner.

French Knot
Bring the needle out on the surface of the fabric at the place where the knot is to lie. Wrap the thread around the needle two or three times, depending on how big you want the knot to be. Insert the needle close to where it came out. Holding the knot in place, pull the needle to the wrong side to secure the knot.

Over-sew
Sew the two edges together with close stitches that pass over them both approximately 1/8 in (3 mm) from the edge of both edges.

Satin Stitch
Work parallel straight stitches, close together, across the entire area of a shape to fill it.

Stem Stitch
Bring the needle to the front at the left-hand side of the working line. With the thread beneath the needle, take it through to the back just beneath the working line. Pull the needle through. The thread at this point creates a very slight diagonal to the working line. Continue making these diagonal stitches along the working line, keeping all the stitches the same size.

Yarn Information

ADRIAFIL
- **Angora Carezza DK/ wool/nylon mix,** 1³/₄oz/50g ball, each approx 90yd/83m

ANCHOR
- **Tapisserie Wool,** ¹/₆oz/5g skein, each approx 11yd/10m

ARTESANO
- **Alpaca,** 1³/₄oz/50g ball, each approx 90yd/83m

BERGERE DE FRANCE
- **Doussine,** 1³/₄oz/50g ball, each approx 174yd/160m

BROWN SHEEP COMPANY
- **Cotton Fleece,** 4oz/113g ball, each approx 215yd/238m
- **Lambs Pride Worsted,** 4oz/113g ball, each approx 190yd/174m

COTTAGE KNITS
- **Chenille,** 1³/₄oz/50g ball, each approx 100yd/92m

DEBBIE BLISS YARNS
- **Baby Cashmerino,** 1³/₄oz/50g ball, each approx 136yd/125m
- **Cashmerino Aran,** 1³/₄oz/50g ball, each approx 98yd/90m
- **Cashmerino Astrakhan,** 1³/₄oz/50g ball, each approx 76yd/70m
- **Cashmerino Chunky,** 1³/₄oz/50g ball, each approx 76yd/70m
- **Cotton Denim Aran,** 1³/₄oz/50g ball, each approx 74yd/68m

FROG TREE
- **Chunky,** 1³/₄oz/50g ball, each approx 54yd/50m

GGH
- **Big Easy,** 1³/₄oz/50g ball, each approx 77yd/71m
- **Samoa-Mouline,** 1³/₄oz/50g ball, each approx 104yd/95m

JAEGER
- **Aqua Cotton,** 1³/₄oz/50g ball, each approx 116yd/106m
- **Baby Merino 4 ply,** 1³/₄oz/50g ball, each approx 200yd/183m
- **Natural Fleece,** 1³/₄oz/50g ball, each approx 93yd/85m
- **Pure Cotton DK,** 1³/₄oz/50g ball, each approx 116yd/106m
- **Roma,** 1³/₄oz/50g ball, each approx 137yd/125m

JO SHARP YARNS
- **Kid Mohair,** 1³/₄oz/50g ball, each approx 95yd/87m

KARABELLA
- **Aurora Bulky,** 1³/₄oz/50g ball, each approx 56yd/51m
- **Vintage Cotton,** 1³/₄oz/50g ball, each approx 100yd/92m
- **Vintage Mercerised Cotton,** 1³/₄oz/50g ball, each approx 140yd/130m

KING COLE
- **Merino Blend DK,** 1³/₄oz/50g ball, each approx 124yd/112m

LOBSTER POT
- **Bulky,** 3¹/₂ oz/100g ball, each approx 115yd/106m

LOUISA HARDING
- **Kashmir DK,** 1³/₄oz/50g ball, each approx 130yd/119m

OPAL
- **Uni 4ply,** 1³/₄oz/50g ball, each approx 460yd/425m

ROOSTER
- **Almerino DK,** 1³/₄oz/50g ball, each approx 124yd/112.5m

ROWAN
- **All Seasons Cotton,** 1³/₄oz/50g ball, each approx 97.5yd/90m
- **Big Wool,** 1³/₄oz/50g ball, each approx 87yd/80m
- **Kid Silk Haze,** 1³/₄oz/50g ball, each approx 229yd/210m
- **Lurex Shimmer,** ³/₄oz/25g ball, each approx 104yd/95m
- **Soft Baby,** 1³/₄oz/50g ball, each approx 164yd/150m
- **Summer Tweed Aran,** 1³/₄oz/50g ball, each approx 118yd/108m
- **4ply Cotton,** 1³/₄oz/50g ball, each approx 186yd/170m

Yarn Resources

RYC
- **Cashcotton 4 ply,** 1¾oz/50g ball, each approx 197yd/180m
- **Cashsoft 4 ply,** 1¾oz/50g ball, each approx 197yd/180m
- **Cashsoft Aran,** 1¾oz/50g ball, each approx 95yd/87m
- **Cashsoft DK (light worsted),** 1¾oz/50g ball, each approx 142yd/130m
- **Luxury Cotton DK,** 1¾oz/50g ball, each approx 104yd/95m
- **Silk Wool DK,** 1¾oz/50g ball, each approx 109yd/100m

SIRDAR
- **Bonus Chunky,** 3½oz/100g ball, each approx 149yd/137m
- **Breeze,** 1¾oz/50g ball, each approx 288yd/264m
- **Chunky,** 1¾oz/50g ball, each approx 64yd/58m
- **Snuggly DK,** 1¾oz/50g ball, each approx 249yd/276m

TWILLEYS
- **Freedom Cotton DK,** 1¾oz/50g ball, each approx 55yd/50m

ADRIAFIL
c/o www.plymouthyarn.com

ANCHOR
c/o www.westminsterfibers.com

ARTESANO
www.artesano.co.uk

BERGERE DE FRANCE
c/o www.angelyarns.com

BROWN SHEEP COMPANY
www.brownsheep.com

COTTAGE KNITS
www.cottageknits.com

DEBBIE BLISS
c/o www.knittingfever.com

FROG TREE
c/o www.kyarns.com

GGH
c/o www.muenchyarns.com

JAEGER
See Anchor

JO SHARP
www.josharp.com.au

KARABELLA
www.karabellayarns.com

KING COLE
www.kingcole.co.uk

LOBSTER POT
c/o www.kyarns.com

OPAL
www.ptyarn.com

ROOSTER
www.roosteryarns.com

ROWAN
See Anchor

RYC
See Anchor

SIRDAR
See Debbie Bliss

TWILLEYS
www.twilleys.co.uk

I would like to extend a huge thank you to Michelle Lo and Katie Cowan for inviting me to do this book, and lighting my creative flair!

Also, a huge thank you to the wonderful team at Collins & Brown, in particular Gemma Wilson, Ben and Ruth, Mark Winwood for his ability to make toys come to life, Amy, Komal, Joanna and Laura! Add to this a special big cheer to kindly Katie Hudson with her gentle liaising and infectious enthusiasm.

It is really great to know and work with you all.